Be Thou an Example

Be Thou an Example

Gordon B. Hinckley

Deseret Book Company
Salt Lake City, Utah
1981

©1981 Deseret Book Company
All rights reserved
Printed in the United States of America
ISBN 0-87747-899-6

First printing November 1981

Library of Congress Cataloging in Publication Data

Hinckley, Gordon Bitner, 1910-
    Be thou an example.

    Includes index.
    1. Church of Jesus Christ of Latter-day Saints—
Doctrinal and controversial works—Addresses, essays,
lectures. 2. Christian life—Mormon authors—Addresses,
essays, lectures. I. Title.
BX8637.H5   230'.933   81-15109
ISBN 0-87747-899-6   AACR2

CONTENTS

Be thou an example
of the believers,
in word,
in conversation,
in charity,
in spirit,
in faith,
in purity.

— 1 Timothy 4:12

Part I

Our Personal

Example

1

THE TRUE STRENGTH
OF THE CHURCH

Mine has been the opportunity to meet many wonderful men and women in various parts of the
world. A few of them have left an indelible impression upon
me. One such person was a naval officer from Asia, a brilliant
young man who had been brought to the United States for ad-
vanced training. Some of his associates in the United States
Navy, whose behavior had attracted him, shared with him at
his request their religious beliefs. He was not a Christian, but
he was interested. They told him of the Savior of the world, of
Jesus born in Bethlehem, who gave his life for all mankind.
They told him of the appearance of God, the Eternal Father,
and the resurrected Lord to the boy Joseph Smith. They spoke
of modern prophets. They taught him the gospel of the Master.
The Spirit touched his heart, and he was baptized.

He was introduced to me just before he was to return to his
native land. We spoke of these things, and then I said, "Your
people are not Christians. You come from a land where Christians have had a difficult time. What will happen when you return home a Christian and, more particularly, a Mormon
Christian?"

His face clouded, and he replied, "My family will be disap-
pointed. I suppose they will cast me out. They will regard me as
dead. As for my future and my career, I assume that all opportunity will be foreclosed against me."

I asked, "Are you willing to pay so great a price for the
gospel?"

His dark eyes, moistened by tears, shone from his handsome brown face as he answered, "It's true, isn't it?"

Ashamed at having asked the question, I responded, "Yes, it's true."

To this he replied, "Then what else matters?"

These are the questions I should like to leave with you: "It's true, isn't it? Then what else matters?"

Some time ago on one of the nation's popular television programs, the Reverend Dean M. Kelley of the National Council of Churches spoke of the declining membership of some of the larger, well-known religious bodies and also of the accelerating growth of others. He gave as the reason for the decline: "Because they have become permissive; they allow just anybody to become members or remain members. They don't insist on any rigorous requirements of belief or of contributions." He pointed out, on the other hand, that those groups which require sacrifice of time and effort and means are enjoying vigorous growth.

He then went on to say: "The fastest growing church [of] over a million members in this country is the Mormon Church, the Latter-day Saints, with headquarters in Salt Lake City, which is growing at five percent a year, [and] that's a very rapid increase."

This is a most striking commentary, and one that should concern every thoughtful man and woman. One thing that it says is that a religion which requires devotion, which asks for sacrifice, which demands discipline, also enjoys the loyalty of its membership and the interest and respect of others.

It was ever thus. The Savior did not equivocate when he said to Nicodemus: "Except a man be born of the water and of the Spirit, he cannot enter into the kingdom of God." (John 3:5.) There were no exceptions. There was no permissiveness in complying with the rule. It was so in other matters of which he spoke.

Paul never hedged nor quibbled when setting forth the requirements of the gospel of Jesus Christ. It is so today. The Lord himself declared that "strait is the gate and narrow is the way." Any system dealing with the eternal consequences of human behavior must set guidelines and adhere to them, and no system can long command the loyalties of men that does not expect of them certain measures of discipline, and particularly of self-discipline. The cost in comfort may be great. The sacrifice may be real. But this very demanding reality is the substance of which character and strength and nobility come.

Permissiveness never produced greatness. Integrity, loyalty, and strength are virtues whose sinews are developed through the struggles that go on within a man as he practices self-discipline under the demands of divinely spoken truth.

But there is another side of the coin, without which this self-discipline is little more than an exercise. Discipline imposed for the sake of discipline is repressive. It is not in the spirit of the gospel of Jesus Christ. It is usually enforced by fear, and its results are negative.

But that which is positive, which comes of personal conviction, builds and lifts and strengthens in a marvelous manner. In matters of religion, when a man is motivated by great and powerful convictions of truth, he disciplines himself—not because of demands made upon him by the Church, but because of the knowledge within his heart that God lives; that he is a child of God with an eternal and limitless potential; that there is joy in service and satisfaction in laboring in a great cause.

The remarkable progress of this church is not so much the result of the requirements of the Church upon its members as it is the result of the conviction in the hearts of those members that this is in very deed the work of God, and that happiness and peace and satisfaction are found in righteous service.

Twice a year we gather on Temple Square in the historic Salt Lake Tabernacle, surrounded by other remarkable buildings, but the strength of the Church is not in these buildings, nor in our thousands of houses of worship across the world, nor in our universities and schools. These are all facilities, desirable, means to an end, but only auxiliary to that which is the true strength. The strength of this church lies in the hearts of its people, in the individual testimony and conviction of the truth of this work. When an individual has that witness and testimony, the requirements of the Church become challenges rather than burdens. Declared the Savior: "My yoke is easy, and my burden is light." (Matthew 11:30.)

The yoke of Church responsibility, the burden of Church leadership become opportunities rather than problems to him who wears the mantle of dedicated membership in the Church of Jesus Christ.

While attending a conference in the East, I listened to the experience of an engineer who had joined the Church some months before. The missionaries had called at his home, and his wife had invited them in. She had eagerly responded to their message, while he felt himself being pulled in against his will. One evening she indicated that she wished to be baptized. He flew into a fit of anger. Didn't she know what this meant? This would mean time. This would mean the payment of tithing. This would mean giving up their friends. This would mean no more smoking. He threw on his coat and walked out into the night, slamming the door behind him. He walked the streets, swearing at his wife, swearing at the missionaries, swearing at himself for ever permitting them to teach them. As he grew tired, his anger cooled, and a spirit of prayer somehow came into his heart. He prayed as he walked. He pleaded with God for an answer to his questions. And then an impression, clear and unequivocal, came almost as if a voice had spoken with words that said, "It's true."

"It's true," he said to himself again and again. "It's true." A peace came into his heart. As he walked toward home, the restrictions, the demands, the requirements over which he had been so incensed began to appear as opportunities. When he opened the door, he found his wife on her knees.

Then, before the congregation to whom he told this, he spoke of the gladness that had come into their lives. Tithing was not a problem; the sharing of their substance with God, who had given them everything, seemed little enough. Time for service was not a problem; this required only a little careful budgeting of the hours of the week. Responsibility was not a problem; out of it came growth and a new outlook on life. And then this man of intellect and training, this engineer, accustomed to dealing with the facts of the physical world in which we live, bore with moistened eyes solemn testimony of the miracle that had come into his life.

So it is with hundreds of thousands in many lands—men and women of capacity and training, of business and the professions, hardheaded, practical men who do things in the work of the world, in whose hearts there burns a silent witness that God lives, that Jesus is the Christ, that this work is divine, that it was restored to earth for the blessing of all who will partake of its opportunities.

Said the Lord: "Behold, I stand at the door, and knock: if any man hear my voice, and open the door, I will come in to him, and will sup with him, and he with me." (Revelation 3:20.)

Jesus, speaking to the Jews in the temple, said: "My doctrine is not mine, but his that sent me. If any man will do his will, he shall know of the doctrine, whether it be of God, or whether I speak of myself." (John 7:16-17.)

This is the wonder of this work, that every man may know for himself. He is not dependent on the teacher or the preacher or the missionary, except as they might instruct and bear witness. As Job declared long ago: "There is a spirit in man: and the inspiration of the Almighty giveth them understanding." (Job 32:8.)

Each man may know for himself, through the gift of the Holy Spirit, that it is true, and with as certain an assurance as that the sun will rise in the morning. And knowing that it is true, he will be inclined to discipline himself as becomes one who has a knowledge of the meaning and purpose of life, of his great responsibility to his fellowmen, of his responsibility to his family, of his responsibility to God.

"Learn of me," said the Lord, "and listen to my words; walk in the meekness of my Spirit, and you shall have peace in me." (D&C 19:23.)

This is the peace "which passeth all understanding," because it comes not of the mind, but of the Spirit, and the things of God are understood by the Spirit of God. (Philippians 4:7; 1 Corinthians 2:11.)

A brilliant and highly educated young woman spoke in

Berchtesgaden, Germany, to a conference of American military personnel who were members of the Church. I was there and heard her. She was a major in the army, a medical doctor, a highly respected specialist in her field. She said:

"More than anything else in the world, I wanted to serve God. But try as I might, I could not find him. The miracle of it all is that he found me. One Saturday afternoon I was at home in Berkeley, California, and heard my doorbell ring. There were two young men there, dressed in suits, with white shirts and ties. Their hair was neatly combed. I was so impressed with them that I said: 'I don't know what you're selling, but I'll buy it.' One of the young men said: 'We aren't selling anything. We're missionaries of The Church of Jesus Christ of Latter-day Saints, and we would like to talk with you.' I invited them to come in, and they spoke about their faith.

"This was the beginning of my testimony. I am thankful beyond words for the privilege and honor of being a member of The Church of Jesus Christ of Latter-day Saints. The joy and peace this glad gospel has brought to my heart are heaven on earth. My testimony of this work is the most precious thing in my life, a gift from my Heavenly Father, for which I will be eternally thankful."

This knowledge comes now just as it came anciently. It so came to my friend, the naval officer from Asia. It so came to the engineer in the East whose words I quoted. It so came to this medical doctor whose testimony I have repeated. Across the world there are now millions who could speak similarly. To those who are searching for the witness of the Holy Spirit in these matters, I give you my testimony that it may be had. It will come now just as it came to Peter of old:

"When Jesus came into the coasts of Caesarea Philippi, he asked his disciples, . . . whom say ye that I am?

"And Simon Peter answered and said, Thou art the Christ, the Son of the Living God.

"And Jesus answered and said unto him, Blessed art thou, Simon Bar-jona: for flesh and blood hath not revealed it unto thee, but my Father which is in heaven.

"And I also say unto thee, That thou art Peter, and upon

this rock I will build my church; and the gates of hell shall not prevail against it." (Matthew 16:13-18.)

This rock of revelation is the source of knowledge concerning the things of God. It is the witness of the Holy Spirit that testifies of eternal truth, and the gates of hell shall not prevail against any man who seeks it, who accepts it, who cultivates it, and who lives by it.

2

CONTEND NOT WITH OTHERS

The days of which our forebears spoke are upon us. These are days of prophecy fulfilled; and I am grateful to be alive and a part of this vibrant, marvelous work which is affecting for good so many people in so many parts of the world. This growth is not a victory of men; it is a manifestation of the power of God. I hope we shall never be proud or boastful concerning it. I pray that we shall ever be humble and grateful.

A most remarkable manifestation occurred on a spring morning in the year 1820 when the Father and the Son appeared to the boy Joseph Smith. All of the good we see in the Church today is the fruit of that remarkable visitation, a testimony of which has touched the hearts of millions in many lands. I add my own witness, given me by the Spirit, that the Prophet's description of that marvelous event is true, that God the Eternal Father and the risen Lord Jesus Christ spoke with him on that occasion in a conversation as real and personal and intimate as are our conversations today. I raise my voice in testimony that Joseph was a prophet, and that the work brought forth through his instrumentality is the work of God.

In 1845, less than a year after Joseph's death, Parley P. Pratt wrote a summary of the Prophet's work and a statement of our obligation to advance it. These words, poetic in their beauty, are as follows:

"He has organized the kingdom of God.—We will extend its dominion.

"He has restored the fulness of the Gospel.—We will spread it abroad.

"He has kindled up the dawn of a day of glory.—We will bring it to its meridian splendor.

"He was a 'little one,' and became a thousand.—We are a small one, and will become a strong nation.

"In short, he quarried the stone. . . . We will cause it to become a great mountain and fill the whole earth." (*Millennial Star* 5 [March 1845]: 151-52.)

We are seeing the unfolding of that dream. I hope we shall be true and faithful to the sacred trust given us to build this kingdom. Our efforts will not be without sorrow and setbacks. We may expect opposition, both determined and sophisticated. As the work grows, we may expect a strengthening of the efforts of the adversary against it. Our best defense is the quiet offense of allegiance to the teachings which have come to us from those whom we have sustained as prophets of God.

Joseph Smith gave us instruction pertinent to the situation in which we find ourselves. Said he, "Go in all meekness, in sobriety, and teach Jesus Christ and him crucified; not to contend with others on account of their faith, or systems of religion, but pursue a steady course. This I delivered by way of commandment, and all who observe it not, will pull down persecution on their heads, while those who do shall always be filled with the Holy Ghost; this I pronounced as a prophecy."

I should like to take a few of the words of that statement as a theme: *Contend not with others, but pursue a steady course.*

We live in a day of shifting values, of changing standards, of will-o'-the-wisp programs that blossom in the morning and die in the evening. We see this in government; we see it in public and private morality; we see it in the homes of the people; we see it in the churches; and we even see it among some of our own members who are led away by the sophistry of men. Men everywhere seem to be groping as men in darkness, casting aside the traditions that were the strength of our society, yet unable to find a new star to guide them.

Some time ago I read a provocative article by Barbara Tuchman, a Pulitzer Prize-winning historian. Said she:

"When it comes to leaders we have, if anything, a super

11

abundance—hundreds of Pied Pipers—ready and anxious to lead the population. They are scurrying around, collecting consensus, gathering as wide an acceptance as possible. But what they are not doing very notably is standing still and saying, 'This is what I believe. This I will do and that I will not do. This is my code of behavior and that is outside it. This is excellent and that is trash.' There is an absence of moral leadership in the sense of a general unwillingness to state standards. . . .

"Of all the ills that our poor . . . society is heir to, the focal one, it seems to me, from which so much of our uneasiness and confusion derive, is the absence of standards. We are too unsure of ourselves to assert them, to stick by them, if necessary in the case of persons who occupy positions of authority, to impose them. We seem to be afflicted by a widespread and eroding reluctance to take any stand on any values, moral, behavioral or esthetic." ("The Missing Element—Moral Courage," *McCall's*, June 1967, p. 28.)

While standards generally may totter, we of the Church are without excuse if we drift in the same manner. We have standards—sure, tested, and effective. To the extent that we observe them, we shall go forward. To the extent that we neglect them, we shall hinder our own progress and bring embarrassment to the work of the Lord. These standards have come from him. Some of them may appear a little out of date in our society, but this does not detract from their validity nor diminish the virtue of their application. The subtle reasoning of men, no matter how clever, no matter how plausible it may sound, cannot abridge the declared wisdom of God.

The patriarch serving in the Milwaukee Stake once spoke a few words that I have not forgotten. Said he: "God is not a celestial politician seeking our vote. Rather, God is to be found, and God is to be obeyed." (Hans Kindt.)

The satisfying thing is that obedience brings happiness; it brings peace; it brings growth—all of these to the individual, and his good example brings respect for the institution of which he is a part.

Our adherence to these divinely given standards need never be an offensive thing to those about us. We need not contend with them. But if we will pursue a steady course, our very example will become the most effective argument we could ever advance for the virtues of the cause with which we are associated.

The Lord has given us counsel and commandment on so many things that no member of this church need ever equivocate. He has established our guidelines concerning personal virtue, neighborliness, obedience to law, loyalty to government, observance of the Sabbath day, sobriety and abstinence from liquor and tobacco, the payment of tithes and offerings, the care of the poor, the cultivation of home and family, the sharing of the gospel, to mention only a few.

There need be nothing of argument or contention in any of them. If we will pursue a steady course in the implementation of our religion in our own lives, we shall advance the cause more effectively than by any other means.

There may be those who will seek to tempt us away. There may be those who will try to bait us. We may be disparaged. We may be belittled. We may be inveighed against. We may be caricatured before the world. There are those, both in the Church and out, who would compel us to change our position on some matters, as if it were our prerogative to usurp authority which belongs to God alone.

We have no desire to quarrel with others. We teach the gospel of peace. But we cannot forsake the word of the Lord as it has come to us through men whom we have sustained as prophets. We must stand and say, to quote again the words of Miss Tuchman: "This is what I believe. This I will do and that I will not do. This is my code of behavior and that is outside it."

There may be times of discouragement and deep concern. There certainly will be days of decision in the lives of each of us. It was ever thus.

Every man and woman in this church knows something of the price paid by our forebears for their faith. I am reminded of this when I read the narrative of my wife's grandmother. She tells of her childhood in Brighton, that delightful city on the south coast of England, where the soft, green hills of Sussex roll down to the sea. It was there that her family were baptized. Their conversion came naturally because the Spirit whispered

13

in their hearts that it was true. But there were critical relatives and neighbors and even mobs to deride and inflame others against them. It took courage, that rare quality described as moral courage, to stand up and be counted, to be baptized and recognized as Mormons.

The family traveled to Liverpool, where with some nine hundred others they boarded the sailing vessel *Horizon*. As the wind caught the sails, they sang "Farewell, My Native Land, Farewell."

After six weeks at sea—to cover the distance covered today by a jet plane in six hours—they landed at Boston and then traveled by steam train to Iowa City for fitting out. There they purchased two yoke of oxen, one yoke of cows, a wagon, and a tent. They were assigned to travel with and assist one of the handcart companies. At Iowa City also occurred their first tragedy. Their youngest child, less than two years of age, suffering from exposure, died and was buried in a grave never again visited by a member of the family.

Now let me give you the very words of this thirteen-year-old girl as I read a few lines from her story:

"We traveled from 15 to 25 miles a day . . . till we got to the Platte River. . . . We caught up with the handcart companies that day. We watched them cross the river. There were great lumps of ice floating down the river. It was bitter cold. The next morning there were fourteen dead. . . . We went back to camp and had our prayers, [and] . . . sang 'Come, Come Ye Saints, No Toil Nor Labor Fear.' I wondered what made my mother cry [that night]. . . . The next morning my little sister was born. It was the 23rd of September. We named her Edith. She lived six weeks and died. . . . [She was buried at the last crossing of the Sweetwater.]

"[We ran into heavy snow. I became lost in the snow.] My feet and legs were frozen. . . . The men rubbed me with snow. They put my feet in a bucket of water. The pain was terrible. . . .

"When we arrived at Devils Gate it was bitter cold. We left many of our things there. . . . My brother James . . . was as well as he ever was when he went to bed [that night]. In the morning he was dead. . . .

14

"My feet were frozen; also my brother's and my sister's. It was nothing but snow [snow everywhere and the bitter Wyoming wind]. We could not drive the pegs in our tents. . . . We did not know what would become of us. [Then] one night a man came to our camp and told us . . . Brigham Young had sent men and teams to help us. . . . We sang songs, some danced and some cried. . . . My mother had never got well. . . . She died between the Little and Big Mountains. . . . She was 43 years of age. . . .

"We arrived in Salt Lake City nine o'clock at night the 11th of December 1856. Three out of the four that were living were frozen. My mother was dead in the wagon. . . . Early next morning Brigham Young came. . . . When he saw our condition, our feet frozen and our mother dead, tears rolled down his cheeks. . . .

"The doctor amputated my toes . . . [while] the sisters were dressing mother for her grave. . . . When my feet were fixed they [carried] . . . us in to see our mother for the last time. Oh, how did we stand it? That afternoon she was buried. . . .

"I have thought often of my mother's words before we left England. 'Polly, I want to go to Zion while my children are small, so they can be raised in the Gospel of Christ, for I know this is the true church.' " (*Life of Mary Ann Goble Pay*.)

I conclude with this question: Should we be surprised if we are called upon to endure a little criticism, to make some small sacrifice for our faith, when our forebears paid so great a price for theirs?

Without contention, without argument, without offense, let us pursue a steady course, moving forward to build the kingdom of God. If there is trouble, let us face it calmly. Let us overcome evil with good. This is God's work. It will continue to strengthen over the earth, touching for good the lives of countless thousands whose hearts will respond to the message of truth. No power under heaven can stop it. This is my faith and this is my testimony. God help us to be worthy of the great and sacred commission that is ours, thus to build his kingdom.

3

"RISE, AND STAND
UPON THY FEET"

In our services we sometimes sing "Come, O thou King of kings!/We've waited long for thee,/With healing in thy wings,/To set thy people free." (*Hymns*, no. 20.) This hymn was written during those troubled years when our forebears were driven and pressed, and when they were winnowed as grain thrown before the wind and tried in the crucible of persecution. They longed for the millennial day when the Lord will come to earth to reign as King of kings.

Theirs was not a hollow dream. The God of heaven has ordained that day. The prophets of all dispensations have spoken of it. We know not when it will come, but its dawning is certain.

We need not wait, however, for that millennial morning. We can improve today without waiting for tomorrow. We can alter circumstances ourselves, without waiting for others. We can hold back the forces that would debilitate and weaken us. We can strengthen the forces that will improve the world.

Reflecting on this, I have thought of the words of Paul to Agrippa when Paul described his experience on the road to Damascus. He saw a light from heaven and heard a voice speaking unto him, and he fell to the ground. And Jesus said, "Rise, and stand upon thy feet: for I have appeared unto thee . . . to make thee a minister and a witness, . . . To open their eyes, and to turn them from darkness to light, and from the power of Satan unto God." (Acts 26:16, 18.)

This is the business of the Church—to open the vision of men to eternal verities and to prompt them to take a stand for equity and decency, for virtue, sobriety, and goodness.

More than a century ago Alex de Tocqueville, a French philosopher, visited America and out of the impressions of that tour wrote these interesting words: "I sought for the greatness and genius of America in her commodious harbors and her ample rivers, and it was not there; in her fertile fields and boundless prairies, and it was not there; in her rich mines and her vast world commerce, and it was not there. Not until I went to the churches of America and heard her pulpits aflame with righteousness did I understand the secret of her genius and power. America is great because she is good, and if America ever ceases to be good, America will cease to be great."

Where has the goodness of America gone? What happened to her pulpits aflame with righteousness? Why are so many of her youth disillusioned and rebellious?

I am not one who believes that all is wrong with this land. There is so much that is right and so much that is good. But neither do I believe that all is well. Our problems are legion, and we are not alone in these. Other lands, most lands, are similarly afflicted.

But this need not be a terminal illness. The course can be changed. We can bring about a regression of the dread disease that seems to trouble us.

Too often we think our society is a vast, impersonal establishment, complex almost beyond comprehension. But although both complex and vast, it is made up of individuals. It was to Saul, the individual, that the Lord spoke on the way to Damascus. Saul's life was changed that day, and thereafter Saul changed the world.

Problems of the kind we have today are not new. Ezekiel cataloged the evils of ancient Israel—immorality, dishonesty, oppression of the poor, robbery, and many others. And then the Lord said through Ezekiel: "I sought for a man among them, that should make up the hedge, and stand in the gap before me

17

for the land, that I should not destroy it." There then follows this tragic conclusion: "but I found none." (Ezekiel 22:30.)

It is better today. There is a man. Yes, there are many men who will build up a wall and stand in the breach against the evils that would erode our society. But there is need for so many more.

The place to begin to reform the world is not Washington or Paris or Tokyo or London. The place to begin is with oneself. A wise man once declared: "Make of yourself an honest man and there will be one fewer rascals in the world."

From self, the next step is the family. The Lord through revelation has laid upon parents the mandate to "teach their children to pray, and to walk uprightly before the Lord." (D&C 68:28.)

Fathers and mothers are needed who will rise and stand upon their feet to make of their homes sanctuaries in which children will grow in a spirit of obedience, industry, and fidelity to tested standards of conduct. If our society is coming apart at the seams, it is because the tailor and the seamstress in the home are not producing the kind of stitching that will hold under stress. In the name of giving advantages, we have too often bartered away the real opportunities of our children.

I once clipped an interesting ad from one of our magazines. It reads as follows:

"I want my boy to have all the advantages I can give him—

"Such as having to earn his own allowance by running errands, cutting lawns.

"Such as getting good grades in school—getting them because he wants to, and because he knows what it would do to me if he didn't.

"Such as being proud to be clean and neat and decent.

"Such as standing up and standing proud when his country's flag goes by.

"Such as addressing elder friends of his parents as 'sir' and 'ma'am.'

"Such as having to earn his own way in the world and knowing he has to prepare for it by hard work, hard study, and sacrificing some of the pleasures and ease his friends may get from too-indulgent parents.

"These are the advantages I want my son to have, because these are the things which will make him self-respecting and self-reliant and successful. And that is the happiness I want him to have." (*U.S. News & World Report,* March 18, 1968, p. 1.)

To this I should like to add that I want my son to have yet other advantages:

I want him to read the great stories of the Old Testament in the very language of the Bible and become acquainted with the great men to whom Jehovah spoke.

I want him to read—along with his science and politics and business—the New Testament, the Gospels with their record of the matchless life of the Son of God, and the writings of the courageous men who testified of him and who sealed their undying witness with their lives.

I want him to read the testament of the New World, the Book of Mormon, as another witness of the divinity and living reality of the Lord Jesus Christ, the Redeemer of mankind.

I want my son to have the advantage of faith in the living God, a faith that will carry him through the inevitable storms and strains of life, a faith that will discipline him against the temptations that will seductively beckon him.

A young man came into my office a few years ago. He was dressed in uniform. He was on his way home from Vietnam. For a year he had walked through the furnace of battle in a hotly contested area along the Laotian border.

I had seen him just before he left for Asia. Now he had come back, alive—miraculously, as he regarded it—thankful, but depressed in spirit.

He had just arrived at the airport and had a little time before his bus left for the small country town where he had grown up and where some of his family still live. We talked about the war. I noticed the campaign ribbons on his chest, including a citation for outstanding service.

I told him the town band would be out to meet him, that he could go home with pride. He looked up and said, "No, I'm ashamed."

"Ashamed of what?" I asked.

"Of what I've done," he replied. "I should have been

19

stronger. I was weak. I gave in, first on little things and then on big ones. Oh, I did nothing that the men all about me were not doing. But I should have done better. My friends back home would have expected better things of me, and had I been stronger I might have helped some of those who, with the right example, would have had the strength to resist."

He lowered his head as we talked, and I saw tears fall from his cheek across the ribbons on his chest.

I tried to reassure him, but he found little comfort. He was a military hero, but he regarded himself as a moral coward.

Not long after that I talked with another young man also recently returned from the war. He too had walked the jungle patrols, his heart pounding with fear. But reluctantly he admitted that the greatest fear he had was the fear of ridicule.

The men of his company laughed at him, taunted him, plastered him with a nickname that troubled him. They told him they were going to force him to do some of the things they reveled in. Then on one occasion when the going was rough, he faced them and quietly said, "Look, I know you think I'm a square. I don't consider myself any better than any of the rest of you. But I grew up in a different way. I grew up in a religious home and a religious town. I went to church on Sundays. We prayed together as a family. I was taught to stay away from these things. It's just that I believe differently. With me it's a matter of religion, and it's kind of a way of respecting my mother and my dad. All of you together might force me toward a compromising situation, but that wouldn't change me, and you wouldn't feel right after you'd done it."

One by one they silently turned away. But during the next few days each came to ask his pardon, and from his example others gained the strength and the will to change their own lives. He taught the gospel to two of them and brought them into the Church.

The difference between these two young men lay in the homes from which they came. The first came from a home where there was bickering, tyranny, drinking, neglect, abandonment, and finally divorce. When the storm of temptation blew against the young tree, the roots were in shallow soil, and it fell.

The second came from the same kind of town—small, dusty, and unimportant. The home from which he came was likewise modest, but a good man presided in that home as the father. He dealt with his wife with kindness, respect, and courtesy. The mother honored her husband and cast an aura of love about the home. And the son who left that home carried with him a fiber in his soul, a fiber that held firm under the tauntings of his associates, whose eyes he opened when he arose and stood on his feet as a quiet witness of the teachings of his parents.

This is the kind of strength that will come from fathers who quietly stand before their families as ministers and witnesses of the eternal verities which, when nurtured in the home, build character in the citizens of the nation.

I repeat, the first place to take a position for right is with oneself. The second is with the family. The third is with the community and the state. Here again there is a call for men and women who will rise and stand against plans and programs that will expose our youth to influences that inevitably will trap some. There are many such influences and programs in every community. May I mention one specifically? I do so because it is an issue that we regard as having serious moral consequences.

No one can honestly doubt that alcohol is a problem in our society. More than 25,000 people die each year on our highways in accidents that are alcohol-related. Drinking is recognized as a factor in a majority of serious crimes. It leaves in its wake a train of evils—broken homes, abandoned children, unemployment, and many other social problems.

The state of Utah has long had one of the lowest per capita consumption rates in the nation, less than half the average of those states that permit the sale of liquor by the drink. Under present law no adult who wants to drink is denied that privilege, and yet there have been proposals, under the guise of better control, to greatly expand the availability of liquor, providing for public bars where people of all ages could be admitted. We are convinced that this would mean a much wider exposure of youth to alcohol, with, as we believe, consequent tragic results. We are not so naive as to think that every young man or woman who happens to be in the vicinity of a public bar would

21

partake of a drink. But we are convinced that the wider the exposure, the more there will be who will partake.

The leadership of a dedicated and concerned handful has grown to an army of many thousands of men and women from all walks of life and from all political parties who have risen and stand in opposition to these efforts. They are men and women of many churches, joining hands in a common cause against a program that would benefit a few at the expense of the many. This is but one example of what can happen when a few men rise and stand for principle. Others follow, a few at first, but the number grows. As in the days of Saul, so it may be in our time. In so standing, we honor a great heritage and leave a greater inheritance. May I close with three questions taken from the Jewish Theological Seminary:

"How shall we pass on our heritage?

"Will it be diminished or increased?

"Will we be the grandfathers, or only the grandsons of great men?"

God bless us with strength to stand for the right.

4

A CITY SET
UPON A HILL

In the fall of 1974, for the better part of a week I stood in the entrance to the Washington Temple as a host to special guests. These included the wife of the president of the United States, justices of the Supreme Court, senators and congressmen, ambassadors from various nations, clergymen, educators, and business leaders. Other visitors, more than 700,000 of them, came to see this sacred edifice.

A vast amount of newspaper and magazine space was given the temple, and radio and television carried its story far and wide. It is doubtful that any building constructed in the East in recent years had attracted so much attention.

Almost without exception, those who came were appreciative and reverent. Many were deeply touched in their hearts. Upon leaving the temple, Mrs. Gerald Ford, wife of the then-president of the United States, commented: "This is a truly great experience for me. . . . It's an inspiration to all."

As I, with others, stood in that sacred edifice day after day shaking hands with many of the honored and respected of this country and of the world, two trains of thought repeatedly crossed my mind. The first concerned the history of the past. The second was occupied with the present and the future.

Watching the First Lady having her photograph taken with President Spencer W. Kimball, my mind drifted back 135 years. Our people were then in Commerce, Illinois, homeless and destitute, facing the bitter winter that soon followed. They had been driven from Missouri and had fled across the Mississippi seeking asylum in Illinois. Where the river makes a wide bend, they had purchased a tract of land, beautiful in its location, but so swampy that a team could not cross it without becoming mired in mud. This site, with tremendous effort and great sacrifice, was to become Nauvoo the beautiful. But in 1839 it was Commerce, a rendezvous for thousands driven from their homes and now homeless. They had left behind the labors of years—houses and barns, churches and public buildings, and hundreds of productive farms. Moreover, buried beneath the Missouri sod, they had left loved ones who had been killed by the mob. Destitute now, and dispossessed, unable to get redress from Missouri, they determined to petition the president and the Congress of the United States. Joseph Smith and Elias Higbee were assigned to go to Washington.

They left Commerce October 20, 1839, riding in a light horse-drawn buggy. They arrived in Washington five weeks later. Much of their first day was spent trying to find accommodations they could afford. They noted in a letter to Hyrum Smith: "We found as cheap boarding as can be had in this city." (*History of the Church* 4:40.)

Calling upon the president of the United States, Martin Van Buren, they stated their case. Responded he: "Gentlemen, your cause is just, but I can do nothing for you. . . . If I take up for you, I shall lose the vote of Missouri." (HC 4:80.)

They then appealed to Congress. In the frustrating weeks that followed, Joseph returned to Commerce, much of the way by horseback. Judge Higbee remained to plead their cause, only to be told finally that Congress would do nothing.

How far the Church has come in the respect and confidence of public officials between 1839, when Joseph Smith was repudiated in Washington, and today, when the president of the Church is welcomed and honored. Such, in essence, were the first and last chapters of my thoughts during those beautiful days at the Washington Temple.

And between those two first and final chapters there ran the thread of a score of other chapters that spoke of the death of Joseph and Hyrum that sultry day of June 27, 1844; of the sacking of Nauvoo; of long trains of wagons crossing the river into Iowa Territory; of the camps in the snows and mud that fateful spring of 1846; of Winter Quarters on the Missouri, and the black canker, the fevers, and the plague that decimated the ranks; of the call for men to join the army, issued by the same government that earlier had been deaf to their pleas; of the grave-marked trail up the Elkhorn, the Platte, and the Sweetwater, over South Pass, and thence to the Salt Lake Valley; of the tens of thousands who left the eastern part of the United States and England to thread their way over that long trail, some pulling handcarts and dying in the Wyoming winter; of the endless grubbing of sagebrush in these valleys; of the digging of miles of ditches to lead water to the thirsty soil; of decades of hue and cry against us, born of bigotry; of the deprivation of rights of citizenship under laws enacted in that same Washington and enforced by marshals sent out from the seat of the federal government. These are among the chapters of that epic history.

Thanks be to God those harsh days are past. Thanks be to those who remained true while walking through those testing fires. What a price, what a terrible price they paid, of which we are the beneficiaries. Thanks for those who through the virtue of their lives have since earned for this people a new measure of respect. Thanks for a better day, with greater understanding and with wide and generous appreciation extended The Church of Jesus Christ of Latter-day Saints.

These were my thoughts as I shook hands with many of the thousands who came to the Washington Temple with curiosity and left with appreciation, some with tears in their eyes.

But those thoughts were largely of the past. There were others of the present and the future. One day while riding along the beltway in the traffic, I looked with wonder, as must all who travel that highway, at the gleaming spires of the Lord's house rising heavenward from a hill in the woods. Words of scripture came into my mind, words spoken by the Lord as he stood upon the mount and taught the people. Said he:

"A city that is set on an hill cannot be hid. Neither do men light a candle, and put it under a bushel, but on a candlestick;

and it giveth light unto all that are in the house. Let your light so shine before men, that they may see your good works, and glorify your Father which is heaven." (Matthew 5:14-16.)

Not alone the Washington Temple, but this entire people have become as a city upon a hill that cannot be hid.

Sometimes we take offense when one who is nominally a member of the Church is involved in a crime and the public press is quick to say that he is a Mormon. We comment among ourselves that if he had been a member of any other church, no mention would have been made of it.

Is not this very practice an indirect compliment to our people? The world expects something better of us, and when one of our number falters, the press is quick to note it. We have, indeed, become as a city upon a hill for the world to see. If we are to be that which the Lord would have us, we must indeed become "a royal priesthood, an holy nation, a peculiar people; that [we] should shew forth the praises of him who hath called [us] out of darkness into his marvellous light." (1 Peter 2:9.)

Unless the world alters the course of its present trends (and that is not likely); and if, on the other hand, we continue to follow the teachings of the prophets, we shall increasingly become a peculiar and distinctive people of whom the world will take note. For instance, as the integrity of the family crumbles under worldly pressures, our position on the sanctity of the family will become more obvious and even more peculiar in contrast, if we have the faith to maintain that position.

As the growing permissive attitude toward sex continues to spread, the doctrine of the Church, as consistently taught for more than a century, will become increasingly singular and even strange to many.

As the consumption of alcohol increases each year under the mores of our society and the allurements of advertising, our position, set forth by the Lord more than a century ago, will become more unusual before the world.

As government increasingly assumes the burden of caring for all human needs, the independence of our social services, and the doctrine that lies behind that position, will become more and more unique.

As the Sabbath increasingly becomes a day of merchandising, those who obey the precept of the law written by the finger of the Lord on Sinai and reinforced by modern revelation will appear more unusual.

It is not always easy to live in the world and not be a part of it. We cannot live entirely with our own or unto ourselves, nor would we wish to. We must mingle with others. In so doing, we can be gracious. We can be inoffensive. We can avoid any spirit or attitude of self-righteousness. But we can maintain our standards. The natural tendency will be otherwise, and many have succumbed to it.

In 1856, when we were largely alone in these valleys, some thought we were safe from the ways of the world. To such talk, President Heber C. Kimball responded: "I want to say to you, my brethren, the time is coming when we will be mixed up in these now peaceful valleys to that extent that it will be difficult to tell the face of a Saint from the face of an enemy to the people of God. Then, brethren," he went on, "look out for the great sieve, for there will be a great sifting time, and many will fall; for I say unto you there is a test, a *Test*, a TEST coming, and who will be able to stand?" (Orson F. Whitney, *Life of Heber C. Kimball* [Bookcraft, 1945], p. 446.)

I do not know the precise nature of that test. But I am inclined to think the time is here and that the test lies in our capacity to live the gospel rather than adopt the ways of the world.

I do not advocate a retreat from society. On the contrary, we have a responsibility and a challenge to take our places in the world of business, science, government, medicine, education, and every other worthwhile and constructive vocation. We have an obligation to train our hands and minds to excel in the work of the world for the blessing of all mankind. In so doing we must work with others. But this does not require a surrender of standards.

We can maintain the integrity of our families if we will follow the counsel of our leaders. As we do so, those about us will observe with respect and be led to inquire how it is done.

We can oppose the tide of pornography and lasciviousness

that is destroying the very fiber of nations. We can avoid partaking of alcoholic beverages and stand solidly for legislation that will limit points of sale and exposure to its use. As we do so, we shall find others who feel as we do and will join hands in the battle.

We can more fully care for our own who may be in need rather than pass the burden to government, and thereby preserve the independence and dignity of those who must have and are entitled to help.

We can refrain from buying on the Sabbath day. With six other days in the week, none of us needs to buy furniture on Sunday. None of us needs to buy clothing on Sunday. With a little careful planning we can easily avoid the purchase of groceries on Sunday.

As we observe these and other standards taught by the Church, many in the world will respect us and find strength to follow that which they too know is right. And, in the words of Isaiah, "Many people shall go and say, Come ye, and let us go up to the mountain of the Lord, to the house of the God of Jacob; and he will teach us of his ways, and we will walk in his paths." (Isaiah 2:3.)

We need not compromise. We must not compromise.

The candle that the Lord has lighted in this dispensation can become as a light unto the whole world, and others seeing our good works may be led to glorify our Father in heaven and emulate in their own lives the examples they may have observed in ours.

Said one of the leaders of our nation as he left the Washington Temple and looked up to its spires, "This beautiful structure is a symbol of those virtues which have made us a great nation and a great people. We need such symbols."

There can be many more such symbols than the temple in Washington, and even more impressive ones. Beginning with you and me, there can be an entire people who by the virtue of our lives in our homes, in our vocations, even in our amusements, can become as a city upon a hill to which men may look and learn, and an ensign to the nations from which the people of the earth may gather strength.

5

THE FORCE
OF FAMILY PRAYER

At a newsstand I walked about observing the magazines, intrigued by the number of publications devoted to the restyling and beautification of our homes. Their
titles alone were enough to excite the imagination in the direction of improvement, and their contents indicated a most compelling display of suggestions on how to dress up the old place or
plan for a new one.

Then my eyes drifted to the news magazines. Boldly printed
on the cover of one of these was a shocking question: "Will city
streets ever be safe again?" Inside I read a provocative interview
between the editors of the magazine and the president of the In-
ternational Association of Chiefs of Police, Stanley R.
Schrotel of Cincinnati. The interview described what we have
read so frequently of late—the rising tide of assault, robbery,
and other serious crimes inflicted on unsuspecting people by
criminals, who, for the most part, are young men, many of
them yet in their teens. News stories indicate that one cannot
safely walk the streets of some of our proudest cities. This is not
only in the United States; the same problem is also felt across
the world.

I quote from the interview with Chief Schrotel:

"Q. Are you saying that parents are to blame, really, for
juvenile delinquency?"

"A. I'd have to say that there is a woeful need today for greater strength in the home, greater respect for parents as the authority symbol, and more parental guidance."

I find only one interpretation of this—serious failure in the homes of the people. There is failure in cultivating those virtues which lead to respect for law, respect for associates, even respect for self.

Other symptoms, less dramatic but equally far-reaching in their consequences, are found in the rising toll of domestic tragedies, the broken homes, the children cast adrift from the ties that should give security and stability to their lives. Add to this the cases of warped integrity, of malfeasance, of dereliction of duty, and we have a sordid and miserable picture.

Paul of old declared to Timothy: "This know also, that in the last days perilous times shall come." He said nothing of atomic bombs or intercontinental missiles or death-dealing submarines. Rather, the times shall be perilous because "men shall be lovers of their own selves, . . . blasphemers, disobedient to parents, unthankful, . . . without natural affection, . . . despisers of those that are good." (2 Timothy 3:1-3.)

The police chief listed some of the things he would do to curb this distressing problem. He included stricter law enforcement and more prison sentences. I would not presume to question his formula as an expediency, but I think it is not a basic and enduring solution. The tide will be turned only as the principles governing the behavior of the people are altered.

Honesty, character, and integrity do not come of legislation or police action. Only as we build back into the fiber of our lives the virtues that are the essence of true civilization will the pattern of our times change. That building process must begin in the homes of the people. It must begin with recognition of God as our Eternal Father and of our relationship to him as his children, with communication with him in recognition of his sovereign position, and in supplication for his guidance in our affairs.

Prayer, family prayer in the homes of this and other lands, is one of the simple medicines that would check the dread disease that has eroded the fiber of our character. It is as simple as sunshine and would be as effective in curing our malady. We could not expect a miracle in a day, but in a generation we would have a miracle.

A generation or two ago family prayer in the homes of Christian people throughout the world was as much a part of the day's activity as was eating. As that practice has diminished, our moral decay has ensued.

I feel satisfied that there is no adequate substitute for the morning and evening practice of kneeling together—father, mother, and children. This, more than heavy carpets, more than lovely draperies, more than cleverly balanced color schemes, is the thing that will make for better and more beautiful homes.

There is something in the very posture of kneeling that contradicts the attitudes described by Paul: "proud, . . . heady, highminded."

The very practice of father and mother and children kneeling together evaporates others of those qualities he described: "disobedient to parents, without natural affection." (2 Timothy 3:2-4.)

There is something in the act of addressing the Deity that offsets a tendency toward blasphemy and toward becoming lovers of pleasure more than lovers of God.

The inclination to be unholy, as Paul described it, to be unthankful, is erased as together the family members thank the Lord for life and peace and all that they have.

The scripture declares: "Thou shalt thank the Lord thy God in all things." And again: " . . . in nothing doth man offend God, or against none is his wrath kindled, save those who confess not his hand." (D&C 59:7, 21.)

In remembering together before the Lord the poor, the needy, and the oppressed, there is developed, unconsciously but realistically, a love for others above self, a respect for others, a desire to serve the needs of others. One cannot ask God to help a neighbor in distress without feeling motivated to do something toward helping that neighbor. What miracles would happen in the lives of the children of America, and of the world, if they would lay aside their own selfishness and lose themselves in the service of others. The seed from which this sheltering and fruitful tree may grow is best planted and nurtured in the daily supplications of the family.

I know of no better way to inculcate love for country than for parents to pray before their children for the president and the congress or the queen and the parliament of the land of their citizenship.

On billboards in some of our cities a statement read, "A nation at prayer is a nation at peace." I believe this. I hope this is more than a catchy motto. I am satisfied that we shall not have peace unless and until we request it in the name of the Prince of Peace.

I know of nothing that will ease family tensions, that in a subtle way will bring about the respect for parents which leads to obedience, that will affect the spirit of repentance which will largely erase the blight of broken homes, than will praying together, confessing weaknesses together before the Lord, and invoking the blessings of the Lord upon the home and those who dwell there.

I have been impressed by a statement made by James H. Moyle, who wrote to his grandchildren concerning the family prayer of his own home: "We have not gone to bed before kneeling in prayer to supplicate divine guidance and approval. Differences may arise in the best governed families, but they will be dissipated by the . . . spirit of prayer. . . . Its very psychology tends to promote the more righteous life among men. It tends to unity, love, forgiveness, to service."

In 1872 Colonel Thomas L. Kane, the great friend of the Latter-day Saints in the days of their distress in Iowa and at the time of the coming of the army to the Salt Lake Valley, came west again with his wife and two sons. They traveled to St. George with Brigham Young, stopping each night in the homes along the way. Mrs. Kane wrote a series of letters to her father back in Philadelphia. In one of these she said:

"At every one of the places we stayed on this journey we had prayers immediately after the dinner-supper, and prayers again before breakfast. No one was excused. . . . The Mormons . . . kneel at once, while the head of the household, or an honored guest prays aloud. . . . They spend very little time in ascriptions, but ask for what they need, and thank Him for what He has given. . . . [They] take it for granted that God knows our familiar names and titles, and will ask a blessing on [a particular individual by name], . . . I liked this when I became used to it."

Oh, that we as a people might cultivate this practice, which was of such importance to our pioneer forebears. Family prayer was as much a part of their worship as were the meetings convened in the Salt Lake Tabernacle. With the faith that came of these daily invocations, they grubbed the sagebrush, led the waters to the parched soil, made the desert blossom, governed their families in love, lived in peace one with another, and made their names immortal as they lost themselves in the service of God.

We have reached the tragic point in our history where evidently we cannot invoke the blessings of God in our schools, but we can pray in our homes. The family is the unit of society. The praying family is the hope of a better society. "Seek ye the Lord while he may be found." (Isaiah 55:6.)

Some time ago I was touched by the heartbreaking statement of a young missionary in Japan. He said, "I have been here for months. I can't learn the language. I dislike the people. I am depressed by day and weep at night. I wrote my mother and pleaded for an excuse to return home. I have her reply. She says: 'We're praying for you. There is not a day passes that all of us do not kneel together in the morning before we eat, and in the evening before we retire, and plead with the Lord for his blessing upon you. We have added fasting to our prayer, and when your younger brothers and sisters pray they say, "Heavenly Father, bless Johnny in Japan and help him to learn the language and do the work he was called to do." ' "

This young man then went on to say through his tears, "I will try again. I will add my prayers to theirs and my fasting to their fasting."

Four months later he wrote a letter in which he said, "A miracle has happened. The language has come to me as a gift from the Lord. I have learned to love the people in this beautiful land. God be thanked for the prayers of my family."

Can we make our homes more beautiful? Yes, through addressing ourselves as families to the source of all true beauty. Can we strengthen our society and make it a better place in which to live? Yes, by strengthening the virtue of our family life through kneeling together and supplicating the Almighty in the name of his Beloved Son.

This simple practice, a return to family worship, spreading across the land and over the earth, would in a generation largely lift the blight that is destroying us, and it would restore integrity, mutual respect, and a spirit of thankfulness in the hearts of the people.

6

"BEHOLD YOUR LITTLE ONES"

We took some of our grandchildren to the circus one evening. I was more interested in watching them and many others of their kind than in watching the man on the flying trapeze. I looked at them in wonder as they alternately laughed and stared wide-eyed at the exciting things before them. And I thought of the miracle of children, who become the world's constant renewal of life and purpose. Observing them in the intensity of their interest, even in this atmosphere, my mind reverted to that beautiful and touching scene recorded in the book of Third Nephi when the resurrected Lord took little children in his arms and wept as he blessed them and said to the people, "Behold your little ones." (17:23.)

It is so obvious that the great good and the terrible evil in the world today are the sweet and the bitter fruits of the rearing of yesterday's children. As we train a new generation, so will the world be in a few years. If you are worried about the future, then look to the upbringing of your children. Wisely did the writer of Proverbs declare, "Train up a child in the way he should go: and when he is old, he will not depart from it." (Proverbs 22:6.)

When I was a boy, we lived in the summer on a fruit farm. We grew great quantities of peaches—carloads of them. Our father took us to tree pruning demonstrations put on by the Agricultural College. Each Saturday during January and February we would go out to the farm and prune the trees. We learned that by clipping and sawing in the right places, even when snow was on the ground and the wood appeared dead, we could shape a tree so that the sun would touch the fruit that was to come with spring and summer. We learned that in February we could pretty well determine the kind of fruit we would pick in September.

E. T. Sullivan once wrote these interesting words: "When God wants a great work done in the world or a great wrong righted, he goes about it in a very unusual way. He doesn't stir up his earthquakes or send forth his thunderbolts. Instead, he has a helpless baby born, perhaps in a simple home out of some obscure mother. And then God puts the idea into the mother's heart, and she puts it into the baby's mind. And then God waits. The greatest forces in the world are not the earthquakes and the thunderbolts. The greatest forces in the world are babies." (*The Treasure Chest,* p. 53.)

And those babies, I should like to add, will become forces for good or ill, depending in large measure on how they are reared. The Lord, without equivocation, has declared, "I have commmanded you to bring up your children in light and truth." (D&C 93:40.)

If I may be pardoned for suggesting the obvious, I do so only because the obvious is not observed in so many instances. The obvious includes four imperatives with reference to children: Love them. Teach them. Respect them. Pray with them and for them.

There is a bumper sticker seen much of late that asks the question, "Have you hugged your child today?" How fortunate, how blessed is the child who feels the affection of his parents. That warmth, that love will bear sweet fruit in the years that follow. In large measure the harshness that characterizes so much of our society is an outgrowth of harshness imposed on children years ago.

When I met one of my childhood friends one day, there came a train of memories of the neighborhood in which we grew up. It was a microcosm of the world, with many varieties of people. They were a close-knit group, and I think we knew them all. I think, also, we loved them all—that is, except for one man. I must make a confession: I detested that man. I have since repented of that emotion, but as I look back, I can sense again the intensity of my feeling. His young boys were our friends, but he was my enemy. Why this strong antipathy? Because he whipped his children with strap or stick or whatever came to hand as his vicious anger flared on the slightest provocation.

Perhaps I disliked the man so much because of the home in which I lived, where there was a father who, by some quiet magic, was able to discipline his family without the use of any instrument of punishment, though on occasion they may have deserved it.

I have seen the fruits of that neighbor's temper come alive again in the troubled lives of his children. I have since discovered that he was one of that very substantial body of parents who seem incapable of anything but harshness toward those for whose coming into the world they are responsible. I have also come to realize that this man, who walks in the memories of my childhood, is but an example of uncounted thousands across the world who are known as child abusers. Every social worker, every duty officer in the emergency room of a large hospital, every policeman and judge in a large city can tell you of them. The whole tragic picture is one of beatings, kickings, slamming, and even sexual assault on small children. And akin to these are those vicious men and women who exploit children for pornographic purposes.

I have no disposition to dwell on this ugly picture. I wish only to say that no man who is a professed follower of Christ and no man who is a professed member of this church can engage in such practices without offending God and repudiating the teachings of his Son. It was Jesus himself who, while holding before us the example of the purity and innocence of children, declared, "Whoso shall offend one of these little ones, . . . it were better for him that a millstone were hanged about his neck, and that he were drowned in the depth of the sea." (Matthew 18:6).

Could there be a stronger denunciation of those who abuse children than these words spoken by the Savior of mankind? Do you want a spirit of love to grow in the world? Then begin within the walls of your own home. Behold your little ones and see within them the wonders of God, from whose presence they have recently come.

Brigham Young once said: "A child loves the smiles of its mother, but hates her frowns. I tell the mothers not to allow the children to indulge in evils, but at the same time to treat them with mildness." (*Discourses of Brigham Young*, p. 323.) He further stated, "Bring up your children in the love and fear of the Lord; study their dispositions and their temperaments, and deal with them accordingly, never allowing yourself to correct them in the heat of passion; teach them to love you rather than to fear you." (Ibid., p. 320.)

Of course, there is need for discipline with families. But discipline with severity, discipline with cruelty, inevitably leads not to correction, but rather to resentment and bitterness. It cures nothing and only aggravates the problem. It is self-defeating. The Lord, in setting forth the spirit of governance in his church, has also set forth the spirit of governance in the home in these great words of revelation:

"No power or influence can or ought to be maintained . . . , only by persuasion, by long-suffering, by gentleness and meekness, and by love unfeigned; Reproving betimes with sharpness, when moved upon by the Holy Ghost; and then showing forth afterwards an increase of love toward him whom thou hast reproved, lest he esteem thee to be his enemy; That he may know that thy faithfulness is stronger than the cords of death." (D&C 121:41, 43-44.)

Behold your little ones and teach them. I need not remind you that your example will do more than anything else in impressing upon their minds a pattern of life. It is always interesting to meet the children of old friends and to find in another generation the ways of their fathers and mothers.

The story is told that in ancient Rome a group of women were, with vanity, showing their jewels one to another. Among them was Cornelia, the mother of two boys. One of the women said to her, "And where are your jewels?" Cornelia responded, pointing to her sons, "These are my jewels." Under her tutelage, and walking after the virtues of her life, they grew to become Gaius and Tiberius Gracchus—the Gracchi, as they were called—two of the most persuasive and effective reformers in Roman history. For as long as they are remembered and spoken of, the mother who reared them after the manner of her own life will be remembered and spoken of with praise also.

May I return again to the words of Brigham Young: "Let it be your constant care that the children that God has so kindly given you are taught in their early youth the importance of the oracles of God, and the beauty of the principles of our holy religion, that when they grow to the years of man and womanhood they may always cherish a tender regard for them and never forsake the truth." (*Discourses of Brigham Young*, p. 320.)

I recognize that there are parents who, notwithstanding an outpouring of love and a diligent and faithful effort to teach them, see their children grow in a contrary manner and weep while their wayward sons and daughters willfully pursue courses of tragic consequence. For such I have great sympathy, and to them I am wont to quote the words of Ezekiel: "The son shall not bear the iniquity of the father, neither shall the father bear the iniquity of the son." (Ezekiel 18:20.)

But such is the exception rather than the rule. Nor does the exception justify others of us from making every effort in showing forth love, example, and correct precept in the rearing of those for whom God has given us sacred responsibility.

Nor let us ever forget the need to respect these, our little ones. Under the revealed word of the Lord, we know they are children of God as we are children of God, deserving of that respect which comes of knowledge of that eternal principle. In fact, the Lord made it clear that unless we develop in our own lives that purity, that lack of guile, that innocence of evil, we cannot enter into his presence. Declared he, "Except ye be converted, and become as little children, ye shall not enter into the kingdom of heaven." (Matthew 18:3.)

Channing Pollock once wrote these interesting and provocative words: "Contemplating the adolescence through which we scorned the wrong, some of us must wish . . . that we could be born old, and grow younger and cleaner and ever simpler and more innocent, until at last, with the white souls of little children, we lay us down to eternal sleep." ("The World's Slow Stain," *Reader's Digest*, June 1960, p. 77.)

Behold your little ones. Pray with them. Pray for them and bless them. The world into which they are moving is a complex and difficult world. They will run into heavy seas of adversity. They will need all the strength and all the faith you can give them while they are yet near you. And they also will need a greater strength that comes of a higher power. They must do more than go along with what they find. They must lift the world, and the only levers they will have are the example of their own lives and the powers of persuasion that will come of their testimonies and their knowledge of the things of God. They will need the help of the Lord. While they are young, pray with them that they may come to know that source of strength which shall then always be available in every hour of need.

I love to hear children pray. I appreciate hearing parents pray for their children. I stand reverently before a father who in the authority of the holy priesthood lays his hands upon the head of a son or daughter at a time of serious decision and in the name of the Lord and under the direction of the Holy Spirit gives a father's blessing.

How much more beautiful would be the world and the society in which we live if every father looked upon his children as the most precious of his assets, if he led them by the power of his example in kindness and love, and if in times of stress he blessed them by the authority of the holy priesthood. And how much more beautiful would be our world and our society if every mother regarded her children as the jewels of her life, as gifts from the God of heaven who is their Eternal Father, and brought them up with true affection in the wisdom and admonition of the Lord.

Said Isaiah of old, "All thy children shall be taught of the Lord; and great shall be the peace of thy children." (Isaiah 54:13.) To this I add, "Great also shall be the peace and the gladness of their fathers and mothers."

7

AN HONEST MAN—
GOD'S NOBLEST WORK

Among many unsigned letters I have received was one of particular interest. It contained a twenty-dollar bill and a brief note that stated that the writer had come to my home many years ago. When there was no response to the bell, he had tried the door and, finding it unlocked, had entered and walked about. He saw a twenty-dollar bill on the dresser, took it, and left. Through the years his conscience had bothered him, and he was now returning the money.

He did not include anything for interest for the period during which he had used this money. But as I read his pathetic letter, I thought of the usury to which he had subjected himself for a quarter of a century with the unceasing nagging of his conscience. For him there had been no peace until he had made restitution.

Our local papers carried a similar story. The state of Utah received an unsigned note together with two hundred dollars. The note read: "The enclosed is for materials used over the years I worked for the state—such as envelopes, paper, stamps, etc."

Imagine the flood of money that would pour into the offices of government, business, and merchants if all who had filched a little here and there were to return that which they had dishonestly taken. The cost of every bag of groceries at the supermarket, of every tie or blouse bought at the shopping center, includes for each of us the burden of shoplifting.

How cheaply some men and women sell their good names! I

recall the widely publicized case of a prominent public figure who was arrested for taking an item costing less than five dollars. I do not know whether he was ever convicted in the courts, but his petty misdeed convicted him before the people. In a measure, at least, his foolish act nullified much of the good he had done and was capable of yet doing.

Each time we board a plane we pay a premium so that our persons and our baggage may be searched in the interest of security. In the aggregate this amounts to millions of dollars, all because of the frightening dishonesty of a few who by threat and blackmail would try to obtain that to which they are not entitled.

One of our national magazines not long ago featured an account of fraud running into the billions in connection with Medicaid. Implicated were some patients, hospitals, clinics, laboratories, and even doctors—all after a dishonest dollar. Padded insurance claims, padded expense accounts, bogus checks, forged documents—these are all symptomatic of an epidemic of unbelievable proportions. In most instances the amount involved individually is small, but in total it represents personal dishonesty on a huge scale.

The book of Genesis contains this remarkable statement: "And Abram said to the king of Sodom, I have lift up mine hand unto the Lord, the most high God, the possessor of heaven and earth, that I will not take from a thread even to a shoe-latchet, and that I will not take any thing that is thine." (Genesis 14:22-23.)

Fortunately there are still those who observe such principles of personal rectitude. We once rode a train from Osaka to Nagoya, Japan. At the station were friends to greet us, and in the excitement my wife left her purse on the train. We called the Tokyo station to report it. When the train arrived at its destination some three hours later, the railroad telephoned to say the purse was there. We were not returning via Tokyo, and more than a month passed before it was delivered to us in Salt Lake City. Everything left in the purse was there when it was returned.

Such experiences, I fear, are becoming increasingly rare. In our childhood we were told the stories of George Washington's confessing to chopping down the cherry tree and Abraham Lincoln's walking a great distance to return a small coin to its rightful owner. But clever debunkers in their unrighteous zeal have destroyed faith in such honesty; the media in all too many cases have paraded before us a veritable procession of deception in its many ugly forms.

What was once controlled by the moral and ethical standards of the people, we now seek to handle by public law. And so the statutes multiply; enforcement agencies consume ever-increasing billions, prison facilities are constantly expanded, but the torrent of dishonesty pours on and grows in volume.

Of course, falsehood is not new. It is as old as man. "The Lord said unto Cain, Where is Abel thy brother? And he said, I know not: Am I my brother's keeper?" (Genesis 4:9.)

Asked the prophet Malachi of ancient Israel: "Will a man rob God? Yet ye have robbed me. But ye say, Wherein have we robbed thee? In tithes and offerings. Ye are cursed with a curse: for ye have robbed me, even this whole nation." (Malachi 3:8-9.)

Even following the miracle of Pentecost, deception was manifest among some who had come into the church. Those who were converted sold their lands and brought money and laid it at the apostles' feet.

"But a certain man named Ananias, with Sapphira his wife, sold a possession, and kept back part of the price, his wife also being privy to it, and brought a certain part, and laid it at the apostles' feet.

"But Peter said, Ananias, why hath Satan filled thine heart to lie to the Holy Ghost, and to keep back part of the price of the land? Whiles it remained, was it not thine own? and after it was sold, was it not in thine own power? Why hast thou conceived this thing in thine heart? Thou hast not lied unto men, but unto God.

"And Ananias hearing these words fell down, and gave up the ghost. . . .

"And it was about the space of three hours after, when his wife, not knowing what was done, came in.

"And Peter answered unto her, Tell me whether ye sold the land for so much? And she said, Yea, for so much.

"Then Peter said unto her, How is it that ye have agreed together to tempt the Spirit of the Lord? . . . Then she fell down straightway at his feet, and yielded up the ghost." (Acts 5:1-10.)

In our time those found in dishonesty do not die as did Ananias and Sapphira, but something within them dies. Conscience chokes, character withers, self-respect vanishes, integrity dies.

On Mount Sinai the finger of the Lord wrote the law on tablets of stone: "Thou shalt not steal." (Exodus 20:15.) There was neither enlargement nor rationalization. And then that declaration was accompanied by three other commandments, the violation of each of which involves dishonesty: "Thou shalt not commit adultery." "Thou shalt not bear false witness." "Thou shalt not covet." (Exodus 20:14, 16-17.)

Was there ever adultery without dishonesty? In the vernacular, the evil is described as "cheating." And cheating it is, for it robs virtue, it robs loyalty, it robs sacred promises, it robs self-respect, it robs truth. It involves deception. It is personal dishonesty of the worst kind, for it becomes a betrayal of the most sacred of human relationships and a denial of covenants and promises entered into before God and man. It is the sordid violation of a trust. It is a selfish casting aside of the law of God; and like other forms of dishonesty its fruits are sorrow, bitterness, heartbroken companions, and betrayed children.

"Thou shalt not bear false witness." Dishonesty again. Television carried the story of a woman imprisoned for twenty-seven years, having been convicted on the testimony of witnesses who had now come forth to confess they had lied. I know that this is an extreme case, but are you not acquainted with instances of reputations damaged, of hearts broken, of careers destroyed by the lying tongues of those who have borne false witness?

I recently read a book of history, a long and detailed account of the trickeries practiced by the nations involved in the Second World War. It was entitled *Bodyguard of Lies*, taken from the words of Winston Churchill, who said: "In war-time, truth is so precious that she should always be attended by a bodyguard of lies." (*The Second World War*, vol. 5, *Closing the Ring* [Boston: Houghton Mifflin, 1951], p. 383.) The book dealt with the many deceptions practiced on each side of the conflict. While reading it, one was again led to the conclusion that war is the devil's own game, and that among its most serious victims is truth.

Unfortunately, the easy use of falsehood and deception goes on long after the treaties of peace are signed, and some of those schooled in the art in times of war continue to ply their skills in days of peace. Then, like a disease that is endemic, the evil spreads and grows in virulence.

When the United States was caught in an embarrassing situation and the president failed to speak truthfully to the world, the country's credibility fell so tragically that it has never entirely recovered. What dismal actions we have witnessed in recent times in contrast with the behavior of those Founding Fathers who two centuries ago pledged their lives, their fortunes, and their sacred honor to establish the republic. The years that followed that declaration witnessed the impoverishment and the deaths of many of these signers, but be it said to their eternal glory that not one ever tarnished his sacred honor.

"Thou shalt not covet." Is not covetousness—that dishonest, cankering evil—the root of most of the world's sorrows? For what a tawdry price men of avarice barter their lives! I recently read a book of fiction dealing with the officers of a great financial institution. With the death of the president, a senior vice-president competed for his office. The story is an intriguing account of a man who was honorable and able, but who in his avarice to get ahead compromised principle until he was utterly destroyed, and in the process almost took down to ruin the very institution he sought to lead. The account is fiction, but the histories of business, of government, of institutions of many kinds are replete with instances of covetous men who in their selfish, dishonest upward climb, destroyed others and eventually destroyed themselves.

Good men, well-intentioned men of great capacity, trade

character for trinkets that turn to wax before their eyes and dreams that become only haunting nightmares.

How rare a gem, how precious a jewel is the man or woman in whom there is neither guile nor deception nor falsehood! We have seen in recent years the tragedy of dishonesty as accounts of bribes have been carried on the front pages of the papers of the United States, Japan, and Europe. And as those revelations have cascaded forth we have been reminded of the words of Benjamin Franklin: "A small leak will sink a great ship," and also the words of Andrew Jackson: "No free government can stand without virtue in the people."

Wrote the author of Proverbs:

"These six things doth the Lord hate: yea, seven are an abomination unto him:

"A proud look, a lying tongue, and hands that shed innocent blood,

"An heart that deviseth wicked imaginations, feet that be swift in running to mischief,

"A false witness that speaketh lies, and he that soweth discord among brethren." (Proverbs 6:16-19.)

The appraisal spoken long ago by an English poet is true yet today: "An honest man's the noblest work of God." (Alexander Pope.) Where there is honesty, other virtues will follow.

The final Article of Faith of The Church of Jesus Christ of Latter-day Saints affirms that "we believe in being honest, true, chaste, benevolent, virtuous, and in doing good to all men."

We cannot be less than honest, we cannot be less than true, we cannot be less than virtuous if we are to keep sacred the trust given us. Once it was said among our people that a man's word was as good as his bond. Shall any of us be less reliable, less honest, than our forebears?

To those who are living this principle, the Lord bless you. Yours is the precious right to hold your heads in the sunlight of truth, unashamed before any man. On the other hand, if there be need for reformation, let it begin where we now stand. God will help us if we will seek that strength which comes from him. Sweet then will be our peace of mind. Blessed will be those with whom we live and associate.

8

"OF YOU IT IS REQUIRED
TO FORGIVE"

In April 6, 1980, the Church observed the 150th anniversary of its birth. As we have reached out across a century and a half of history, we have refreshed the remembrance of our past and paid reverent tribute to those who gave so much to make possible that which we enjoy today. There has been stirred within us a spirit of thanksgiving to Almighty God for the wondrous manner in which he has woven the tapestry of his divine purpose. We have been reminded that we are an important part of the fulfillment of a great prophecy.

All of this has been done in the spirit of jubilee. But there is much yet to be done. In ancient Israel each fiftieth year was observed as a jubilee year with remembrance and celebration. But there was also a mandate urging generous forgiveness and a lifting of the hand of oppression.

Now, as we draw the curtain on 150 years of our history, it becomes us as a grateful people to reach out with a spirit of forgiveness and an attitude of love and compassion toward those we have felt may have wronged us.

We have need of this. The whole world has need of it. It is of the very essence of the gospel of Jesus Christ. He taught it. He exemplified it as none other has exemplified it. In the time of his agony on the cross of Calvary, with vile and hateful accusers before him, they who had brought him to this terrible crucifixion, he cried out, "Father, forgive them; for they know not what they do." (Luke 23:34.)

None of us is called on to forgive so generously, but each of us is under a divinely spoken obligation to reach out with pardon and mercy. The Lord has declared in words of revelation: "My disciples, in days of old, sought occasion against one another and forgave not one another in their hearts; and for this evil they were afflicted and sorely chastened.

"Wherefore, I say unto you, that ye ought to forgive one another; for he that forgiveth not his brother his trespasses standeth condemned before the Lord; for there remaineth in him the greater sin.

"I, the Lord, will forgive whom I will forgive, but of you it is required to forgive all men.

"And ye ought to say in your hearts—let God judge between me and thee, and reward thee according to thy deeds." (D&C 64:8-11.)

How much we have need of the application of this God-given principle, repentance. We see the need for it in the homes of the people, where tiny molehills of misunderstanding are fanned into mountains of argument. We see it among neighbors, where insignificant differences lead to undying bitterness. We see it in business associates who quarrel and refuse to compromise and forgive when, in most instances, if there were a willingness to sit down together and speak quietly one to another, the matter could be resolved to the blessing of all. Rather, they spend their days nurturing grudges and planning retribution.

In the first year of the organization of the Church, when the Prophet Joseph Smith was repeatedly arrested and tried on false charges by those who sought to injure him, the Lord said to him through revelation, "Whosoever shall go to law with thee shall be cursed by the law." (D&C 24:17.) I have seen that in our time among some of those who have vindictively pursued their nurtured grudges. Even among some of those who win their contests there appears to be little peace of mind, and while they may have gained dollars, they have lost something more precious.

Guy de Maupassant, the French writer, tells the story of a peasant named Hauchecome who came on market day to the village. While walking through the public square, his eye caught sight of a piece of string lying on the cobblestones. He picked it up and put it in his pocket. His actions were observed by the village harness maker with whom he had previously had a dispute.

Later in the day the loss of a purse was reported. Hauchecome was arrested on the accusation of the harness maker. He was taken before the mayor, to whom he protested his innocence, showing the piece of string that he had picked up. But he was not believed and was laughed at.

The next day the purse was found, and Hauchecome was absolved of any wrongdoing. But, resentful of the indignity he had suffered because of a false accusation, he became embittered and would not let the matter die. Unwilling to forgive and forget, he thought and talked of little else. He neglected his farm. Everywhere he went, everyone he met had to be told of the injustice. By day and by night he brooded over it. Obsessed with his grievance, he became desperately ill and died. In the delirium of his death struggles, he repeatedly murmured, "A piece of string, a piece of string." (*The Works of Guy de Maupassant* [Roslyn, New York: Black's Reader Service], pp. 34-38.)

With variations of characters and circumstances, that story could be repeated many times in our own day. How difficult it is for any of us to forgive those who have injured us. We are all prone to brood on the evil done us. That brooding becomes as a gnawing and destructive canker. Is there a virtue more in need of application in our time than the virtue of forgiving and forgetting? There are those who would look upon this as a sign of weakness. Is it? I submit that it takes neither strength nor intelligence to brood in anger over wrongs suffered, to go through life with a spirit of vindictiveness, to dissipate one's abilities in planning retribution. There is no peace in the nursing of a grudge. There is no happiness in living for the day when you "get even."

Paul speaks of "the weak and beggarly elements" of our

lives. (See Galatians 4:9.) Is there anything more weak or beggarly than the disposition to wear out one's life in an unending round of bitter thoughts and scheming gestures toward those who may have affronted us?

Joseph F. Smith presided over the Church at a time of great bitterness toward our people. He was the target of vile accusations, of a veritable drumbeat of criticism by editorial writers. He was lampooned, cartooned, and ridiculed. Listen to his response to those who made sport of demeaning him: "Let them alone. Let them go. Give them the liberty of speech they want. Let them tell their own story and write their own doom." (*Gospel Doctrine*, p. 339.) And then with an outreaching spirit of forgiving and forgetting, he went ahead with the great and positive work of leading the Church forward to new growth and remarkable accomplishments. At the time of his death, many of those who had ridiculed him wrote tributes of praise concerning him.

Not long ago I listened at length to a couple who sat across the desk from me. There was bitterness between them. I know that at one time their love was deep and true. But each had developed a habit of speaking of the faults of the other. Unwilling to forgive the kinds of mistakes we all make, and unwilling to forget them and live above them with forbearance, they had carped at one another until the love they once knew had been smothered. It had turned to ashes with the decree of a so-called no-fault divorce. Now there is only loneliness and recrimination. I am satisfied that had there been even a small measure of repentance and forgiveness, they would still be together, enjoying the companionship that had so richly blessed their earlier years.

If there be any who nurture in their hearts the poisonous brew of enmity toward another, I plead with you to ask the Lord for strength to forgive. This expression of desire will be of the very substance of your repentance. It may not be easy, and it may not come quickly. But if you will seek it with sincerity and cultivate it, it *will* come. And even though he whom you have forgiven continues to pursue and threaten you, you will know you have done what you could to effect a reconciliation. There will come into your heart a peace otherwise unattainable. That peace will be the peace of Him who said: "For if ye forgive men their trespasses, your heavenly Father will also forgive you: But if you forgive not men their trespasses, neither will your Father forgive your trespasses." (Matthew 6:14-15.)

I know of no more beautiful story in all literature than that found in the fifteenth chapter of Luke. It is the story of a repentant son and a forgiving father. It is the story of the son who wasted his inheritance in riotous living, rejecting his father's counsel, spurning those who loved him. When he had spent all, he was hungry and friendless, and "when he came to himself," he turned back to his father, who, on seeing him afar off, "ran, and fell on his neck, and kissed him." (Luke 15:17, 20.)

I ask you to read that story. Every parent ought to read it again and again. It is large enough to encompass every household, and enough larger than that to encompass all mankind, for are we not all prodigal sons and daughters who need to repent and partake of the forgiving mercy of our Heavenly Father and then follow his counsel?

His Beloved Son, our Redeemer, reaches out to us in forgiveness and mercy, but in so doing he commands repentance. A true and magnanimous spirit of forgiveness will become an expression of that required repentance. Said the Lord:

"Therefore, I command you to repent—repent, lest I smite you by the rod of my mouth, and by my wrath, and by my anger, and your sufferings be sore—how sore you know not, how exquisite you know not, yea, how hard to bear you know not.

"For behold, I, God, have suffered these things for all, that they might not suffer if they would repent;

"But if they would not repent they must suffer even as I;

"Which suffering caused myself, even God, the greatest of all, to tremble because of pain, and to bleed at every pore, and to suffer both body and spirit. . . .

"Learn of me, and listen to my words; walk in the meekness of my Spirit, and you shall have peace in me." (D&C 19:15-18, 23.)

Such is the commandment, and such is the promise of him who, in his great exemplary prayer, pleaded, "Father, . . . forgive our debts, as we forgive our debtors." (Matthew 6:9, 12.)

Are not the words of Abraham Lincoln beautiful which he spoke out of the tragedy of a terrible civil war: "With malice toward none, with charity for all, . . . let us . . . bind up the nation's wounds." (Second Inaugural Address, March 4, 1865.)

As we conclude our great season of jubilee, let us bind up the wounds—oh, the many wounds that have been caused by cutting words, by stubbornly cultivated grievances, by scheming plans to "get even" with those who may have wronged us. We all have a little of this spirit of revenge in us. Fortunately we all have the power to rise above it, if we will "clothe [ourselves] with the bond of charity, as with a mantle, which is the bond of perfectness and peace." (D&C 88:125.)

"To err is human, to forgive divine." (Alexander Pope, *An Essay on Criticism.*) There is no peace in harboring old grudges. There is no peace in reflecting on the pain of old wounds. There is peace only in repentance and forgiveness. This is the sweet peace of the Christ, who said, "Blessed are the peacemakers; for they shall be called the children of God." (Matthew 5:9.)

9

OPPOSING EVIL

A young man recently came to see me. He was handsome in appearance, a good student, personable, but deeply troubled. He announced that he had long been involved in deviant moral activity but had now come to have serious questions about it.

"What brought this change of attitude?" I asked.

He pointed to a ring on his little finger. It was a beautiful diamond in a heavy gold setting, a handsome ring that he showed me with pride. "It was my grandfather's," he said. "In his old age he gave it to my father, who was his eldest son; and my father gave it to me, his eldest son. The other night I was with a friend of my own kind, and he, knowing the story of my ring, asked, 'To whom will you give it? I guess you're the last one.'

"I was shaken by that," he continued. "I had never thought of it before. 'Where am I going?' I asked myself. 'I am walking down a blind alley, where there is neither light, nor hope, nor future.' I suddenly realized I need help."

We talked of the influences that had put him where he is, of the home from which he came, of associations with other young men, of books and magazines read, of shows seen. He spoke of many friends in similar circumstances or worse.

As I walked from my office toward my home that evening, I

could not get from my mind the tragic figure of that young man now finding himself face to face with the fact that for so long as he continued with his present pattern, he could never have a son of his own to whom he might someday pass his grandfather's ring. The bleakness of his future had brought him pleading for help.

Following dinner, I picked up the morning paper, which I had not previously read. As I thumbed through its pages, my eyes stopped on the theater ads, so many of them an open appeal to witness that which is debauching and which leads to violence and sex.

I turned to my mail and found a small magazine that lists the television fare for the coming week and saw titles of shows aimed in the same direction. A newsmagazine lay on my desk. This particular issue was devoted to the rising crime rate. Articles in the magazine spoke of additional billions for increased police forces and larger prisons.

The flood of pornographic filth and the inordinate emphasis on sex and violence are not peculiar to the United States. The situation is as bad in Europe and in many other areas. News stories tell of the production in Denmark of a filthy, erotic, and blasphemous movie on the life of the Son of God. The whole dismal picture indicates a weakening rot seeping into the very fiber of society.

Our legislatures and courts are affected by this wave. Legal restraints against deviant moral behavior are eroding under legislative enactments and court opinions. This is done in the name of freedom of speech, freedom of the press, freedom of choice in so-called personal matters. But the bitter fruit of these so-called freedoms has been enslavement to debauching habits and behavior that leads only to destruction. A prophet, speaking long ago, aptly described the process when he said, "And thus the devil cheateth their souls, and leadeth them away carefully down to hell." (2 Nephi 28:21.)

On the other hand, I am satisfied that there are millions upon millions of good people in America and in other lands. For the most part, husbands are faithful to wives and wives to husbands. Their children are being reared in sobriety, industry, and faith in God. Given the strength of these, I am one who believes that the situation is far from hopeless. I am satisfied that there is no need to stand still and let the filth and violence overwhelm us, or to run in despair. The tide, high and menacing as it is, can be turned back if enough of the kind I have mentioned will add their strength to the strength of the few who are now effectively working. I believe the challenge to oppose this evil is one from which members of The Church of Jesus Christ of Latter-day Saints, as citizens, cannot shrink. And if we are ever to begin, let it be now.

In that spirit, I should like to suggest four points of beginning:

1. *Begin with yourself.* Reformation of the world begins with reformation of self. It is a fundamental article of our faith that "We believe in being honest, true, chaste, benevolent, and virtuous." (Article of Faith 13.)

We cannot hope to influence others in the direction of virtue unless we live lives of virtue. The example of our living will carry a greater influence than will all the preaching in which we might indulge. We cannot expect to lift others unless we stand on higher ground ourselves.

Respect for self is the beginning of virtue in men. That man who knows that he is a child of God, created in the image of a divine Father and gifted with a potential for the exercise of great and godlike virtues, will discipline himself against the sordid, lascivious elements to which all are exposed. Said Alma to his son Helaman, "Look to God and live." (Alma 37:47.)

It is a matter of more than passing interest that the Lord, as he spoke to the multitude on the Mount, included this marvelous declaration: "Blessed are the pure in heart: for they shall see God." (Matthew 5:8.)

A wise man once said, "Make of yourself an honest man, and there will be one fewer rascals in the world."

And it was Shakespeare who put into the mouth of one of his characters this persuasive injunction: "To thine own self be true,/And it must follow, as the night the day,/Thou canst not then be false to any man." (*Hamlet*, 1, iii, 78-80.)

I should like to give to every member of the Church a challenge to lift his thoughts above the filth, to discipline his acts into an example of virtue, to control his words that he speak only that which is uplifting and leads to growth.

2. *A better tomorrow begins with the training of a better generation.* This places upon parents the responsibility to do a more effective work in the rearing of children. The home is the cradle of virtue, the place where character is formed and habits are established. The home evening is the opportunity to teach the ways of the Lord.

You know that your children will read. They will read books and they will read magazines and newspapers. Cultivate within them a taste for the best. While they are very young, read to them the great stories which have become immortal because of the virtues they teach. Expose them to good books. Let there be a corner somewhere in your house, be it ever so small, where they will see at least a few books of the kind upon which great minds have been nourished.

Let there be good magazines about the house, those which are produced by the Church and by others, which will stimulate their thoughts to ennobling concepts. Let them read a good family newspaper that they may know what is going on in the world without being exposed to the debasing advertising and writing so widely found. When there is a good show in town, go to the theater as a family. Your very patronage will give encouragement to those who wish to produce this type of entertainment. And use that most remarkable of all tools of communication, television, to enrich their lives. There is so much that is good, but it requires selectivity.

Let there be music in the home. If you have teenagers who have their own recordings, you will be prone to describe the sound as something other than music. Let them occasionally hear something better. Expose them to it. It will speak for itself. More of appreciation will come than you may think. It may not be spoken, but it will be felt, and its influence will become increasingly manifest as the years pass.

3. *The building of public sentiment begins with a few earnest voices.* I am not one to advocate shouting defiantly or shaking fists and issuing threats in the faces of legislators. But I *am* one who believes that we should earnestly and sincerely and posi-

tively express our convictions to those given the heavy responsibility of making and enforcing our laws. The sad fact is that the minority who call for greater liberalization, who peddle and devour pornography, who encourage and feed on licentious display make their voices heard until those in our legislature may come to believe that what they say represents the will of the majority. We are not likely to get that which we do not speak up for.

Let our voices be heard. I hope they will not be shrill voices, but I hope we shall speak with such conviction that those to whom we speak shall know of the strength of our feeling and the sincerity of our effort. Remarkable consequences often flow from a well-written letter and a postage stamp. Remarkable results come of quiet conversation with those who carry heavy responsibilities.

Declared the Lord to this people: "Wherefore, be not weary in well-doing, for ye are laying the foundation of a great work. And out of small things proceedeth that which is great. Behold, the Lord requireth the heart and a willing mind." (D&C 64:33-34.)

This is the essence of the matter—"the heart and a willing mind." Speak to those who enact the regulations, the statutes, and the laws—those in government on local, state, and national levels and those who occupy positions of responsibility as administrators of our schools. Of course, there will be some who slam the door, some who will scoff. Discouragement may come. It has always been thus. Edmund Burke, speaking on the floor of the House of Commons in 1783, declared concerning the advocate of an unpopular cause:

"He well knows what snares are spread about his path. . . . He is traduced and abused for his supposed motives. He will remember that obloquy is a necessary ingredient in the composition of all true glory: he will remember . . . that calumny and abuse are essential parts of triumph."

The apostle Paul, in his defense before Agrippa, gave an account of his miraculous conversion while on the way to Damascus, declaring that the voice of the Lord commanded him to "rise, and stand upon thy feet." (Acts 26:16.)

I think the Lord would say to us, "Rise, and stand upon thy

feet, and speak up for truth and goodness, decency and virtue."

4. *Strength to do battle begins with enlisting the strength of God.* He is the source of all true power. Declared Paul to the Ephesians: "Finally my brethren, be strong in the Lord, and in the power of his might. Put on the whole armour of God, that ye may be able to stand against the wiles of the devil. For we wrestle not against flesh and blood, but against principalities, against powers, against the rulers of the darkness of this world, against spiritual wickedness in high places. Wherefore take unto you the whole armour of God, that ye may be able to withstand in the evil day, and having done all, to stand." (Ephesians 6:10-13.)

The tide of evil flows. It has become a veritable flood. Most of us, living somewhat sheltered lives, have little idea of the vast dimensions of it. Billions of dollars are involved for those who pour out pornography, for those who peddle lasciviousness, for those who deal in bestiality, in perversion, in sex and violence. God give us the strength, the wisdom, the faith, the courage as citizens to stand in opposition to these and to let our voices be heard in defense of those virtues which, when practiced in the past, made men and nations strong, and which, when neglected, brought them to decay.

God lives. He is our strength and our helper. As we strive, we shall discover that legions of good men and women will join with us.

10

AND PETER WENT OUT,
AND WEPT

When the Last Supper was concluded, Jesus and his disciples left Jerusalem and went over to the Mount of Olives. Knowing that his terrible ordeal was at hand, he spoke with those he loved. And he said to them: "All ye shall be offended [that is, shall fall away] because of me this night. . . .

"Peter answered and said unto him, Though all men shall be offended because of thee, yet will I never be offended.

"Jesus said unto him, Verily I say unto thee, That this night, before the cock crow, thou shalt deny me thrice.

"Peter said unto him, Though I should die with thee, yet will I not deny thee."

There followed shortly thereafter the terrible agony in the Garden of Gethsemane, and then the betrayal. As the procession moved to the court of Caiaphas, "Peter followed . . . unto the high priest's palace, and went in, and sat with the servants, to see the end."

While the mockery of that trial was going on and Jesus' accusers spit on him, and buffeted him, and smote him with the palms of their hands, a damsel, seeing Peter, said: "Thou also wast with Jesus of Galilee.

"But he denied before them all, saying, I know not what thou sayest.

"And when he was gone out into the porch, another maid saw him, and said unto them that were there, This fellow was also with Jesus of Nazareth.

"And again he denied with an oath, I do not know the man.

"And after a while came unto him they that stood by, and said to Peter, Surely thou also art one of them; for thy speech bewrayeth thee.

"Then began he to curse and to swear, saying, I know not the man. And immediately the cock crew.

"And Peter remembered the word of Jesus, which said unto him, Before the cock crow, thou shalt deny me thrice. *And he went out, and wept bitterly.*" (See Matthew 26:31-75. Italics added.)

What pathos there is in those words! Peter, affirming his loyalty, his determination, his resolution, said that he would never deny. But the fear of men came upon him and the weakness of his flesh overtook him, and under the pressure of accusation, his resolution crumbled. Then, recognizing his wrong and weakness, "he went out, and wept."

As I have read this account, my heart goes out to Peter. So many of us are so much like him. We pledge our loyalty; we affirm our determination to be of good courage; we declare, sometimes even publicly, that come what may, we will do the right thing, we will stand for the right cause, we will be true to ourselves and to others.

Then the pressures begin to build. Sometimes these are social pressures. Sometimes they are personal appetites. Sometimes they are false ambitions. There is a weakening of the will. There is a softening of discipline. There is capitulation. And then there is remorse, self-accusation, bitter tears of regret.

One of the great tragedies we witness almost daily is the tragedy of men of high aim and low achievement. Their motives are noble. Their proclaimed ambition is praiseworthy. Their capacity is great. But their discipline is weak. They succumb to indolence. Appetite robs them of will.

I think of such a man I once knew, not a member of the Church. He was a graduate of a great university. His potential was unlimited. As a young man with an excellent education and a tremendous opportunity, he dreamed of the stars and moved in their direction. In the company that employed him in those early years, he was promoted from one responsibility to another, each with improved opportunity over the last. Before many years had passed, he was in the top echelon of his company. But those promotions brought him into the cocktail circuit. He could not handle it, as so many others cannot. He became an alcoholic, the victim of an appetite he could not control. He sought help but was too proud to discipline himself in the regimen imposed upon him by those who tried to assist him.

He went down like a falling star, tragically burning out and disappearing in the night. I made inquiry of one friend after another, and finally learned the truth of his tragic end. He, who had begun with such high aim and impressive talent, had died on skid row in one of our large cities. Like Peter of old, he had felt certain of his strength and of his capacity to live up to his potential. But he had denied that capacity; and I am confident that as the shadows of his failure closed around him, again like Peter, he must have gone out and wept bitterly.

I think of another. I knew him well. He joined the Church when long ago I was a missionary in the British Isles. He had a smoking habit. He prayed for strength in that springtime of his Church membership and the Lord answered his prayer and gave him power to overcome his habit. He looked to God and lived with a joy he never had previously known. But something happened. Family and social pressures were brought against him. He lowered his vision and gave way to his appetite. The smell of burning tobacco seduced him. I saw him some years later. We talked together of the old and better days he had known. And he, like Peter, wept bitterly. He blamed this and he blamed that, and, as he did so, I was inclined to repeat the words of Cassius: "The fault, dear Brutus, is not in our stars,/ But in ourselves, that we are underlings." (*Julius Caesar*, act 1, sc. 2, lines 140-41.)

And so I might continue telling you of those who begin with noble objectives but then slow down, or of those who are strong starters and weak finishers. So many in the game of life get to first base, or second, or even third, but then fail to score. They are inclined to live unto themselves, denying their generous instincts, grasping for possessions, and, in their self-centered, uninspired living, sharing neither talent nor faith with others. Of them the Lord has said: "And this shall be your lamentation in the day of visitation, and of judgment, and of indignation: The harvest is past, the summer is ended, and my soul is not saved!" (D&C 56:16.)

But more particularly, I wish to say a word concerning those who, like Peter, profess love for the Lord and his work and then, either with voice or by silence, deny him.

I recall so well a young man of great faith and devotion. He was my friend and my mentor during a sensitive period of my life. The manner of his living and the enthusiasm of his service were evidence of his love for the Lord and for the work of the Church. But he was slowly led away by the flattery of associates who saw in him the means of their own advancement in the affairs in which they were engaged together. Rather than lead them in the direction of his own faith and behavior, he slowly succumbed to their enticings in the opposite direction.

He never spoke in defiance of the faith he had lived by. That was not necessary. His altered manner was testimony enough of his having forsaken it. The years passed, and then I met him again. He spoke as one disillusioned. With lowered voice and lowered eyes, he told of his drifting when he cut himself loose from the anchor of his once-treasured faith. Then, concluding his narrative, like Peter, he wept.

Recently I was speaking with a friend concerning a mutual acquaintance, a man looked upon as highly successful in his vocation. "But what of his activity in the Church?" I asked. To this my friend responded, "He knows in his heart that it is true, but he is afraid of it. He is fearful that if he were to acknowledge his Church membership and live its standards, he would be cut off from the social circle in which he moves."

I reflected: Like Peter, who denied his own sure knowledge, the day will come, though possibly not until old age, when in hours of quiet reflection this man will know that he traded his birthright for a mess of pottage. And there will be remorse and sorrow and tears, for he will come to see that he not only denied the Lord in his own life, but also in effect denied him before his children, who have grown up without a faith to cling to.

The Lord himself said, "Whosoever therefore shall be ashamed of me and of my words in this adulterous and sinful generation; of him also shall the Son of man be ashamed, when he cometh in the glory of his Father with the holy angels." (Mark 8:38.)

Now, may I go back to Peter, who denied and wept. Recognizing his error, repenting of his weakness, he turned about and became a mighty voice in bearing witness of the risen Lord. He, the senior apostle, dedicated the remainder of his life to testifying of the mission, the death, and the resurrection of Jesus Christ, the living Son of the living God. He preached the moving sermon on the day of Pentecost when the multitude were touched in their hearts by the power of the Holy Ghost. In the authority of the priesthood received from his Master, he, with John, healed the lame man, the miracle that brought on persecution. He fearlessly spoke for his brethren when they were arraigned before the Sanhedrin. His was the vision that led to carrying the gospel to the Gentiles. (See Acts 2-4, 10.)

He suffered chains and prison and a terrible martyr's death as a witness of Him who had called him from his nets to become a fisher of men. (See Matthew 4:19.) He remained faithful and true to the great and compelling trust given when the resurrected Lord in his final instructions to the eleven apostles charged them to go "and teach all nations, baptizing them in the name of the Father, and of the Son, and of the Holy Ghost." (Matthew 28:19.) And he it was who, with James and John, came back to earth in this dispensation to restore the holy priesthood, under which divine authority the Church of Jesus Christ was organized in these latter days and under which same authority it now functions. These mighty works and many more unmentioned were done by Peter, who once had denied and sorrowed and then rose above that remorse to carry forward the work of the Savior following his ascension and to participate in the restoration of that work in this dispensation.

Now, if there be any today who by word or act have denied

63

the faith, I pray that you may draw comfort and resolution from the example of Peter. So, too, there is a way for you to turn about and add your strength and faith to the strength and faith of others in building the kingdom of God.

May I conclude by telling you about a man I know who grew up with love for the Church. But when he became involved in his business career, obsessed with ambition, he began in effect to deny the faith. The manner of his living became almost a repudiation of his loyalty. Then fortunately, before he had gone too far, he heard the whisperings of the still, small voice. There came a saving sense of remorse. He turned around, and today he stands as the president of a great stake of Zion, while also serving as a senior officer in one of the leading industrial corporations of the nation and of the world.

My beloved brethren and sisters who may also have drifted, the Church needs you, and you need the Church. You will find many ears that will listen with understanding. There will be many hands to help you find your way back. There will be hearts to warm your own. There will be tears, not of bitterness but of rejoicing.

May the Lord touch you by the power of his Spirit to increase your desire. May he strengthen your resolution. May your joy be full and your peace sweet and satisfying as you return to that which you know in your heart is true.

11
EVERYTHING TO GAIN—
NOTHING TO LOSE

The following letter was recently sent to Temple
Square:

Dear Sirs:
I am not of the Mormon religion.
I have never believed in God or Jesus Christ. I have never understood
how to love a spirit that I don't know. When I was baptized, I accepted
Christ because I have always been told that if I wasn't saved, I would go to
hell. Being "saved" has always been thrown at me. I haven't gone to
church in a very long time because I was always being pushed into something I didn't, and still don't, quite understand.
[Someone] showed me a pamphlet, "Man's Search for Happiness,"
and explained what it said. I opened my eyes then, because through the
Mormon religion God made sense to me. . . .
A "small voice" inside of me told me to search for God. Before, it
didn't make any difference to me if God was there or not. Now it does.
Who is God? Why is God? Why does he need or want me? Why am I
here? Why am I so lost? So very, very lost? There are thousands of questions in my head that I want so badly to fulfill with answers. And since I
have no place to go, or I don't know how to start searching, I'm asking you
to give me some understanding of Him and the Mormon religion. Please
help me find my way. Listen to my cry for help and give me sensible
answers. Pamphlets, letters, notes, cards, anything, please.
Thank you so much.

I am satisfied that there are thousands across the world who
in their loneliness and hunger for truth are crying out for help,

as is the writer of that letter. And in addition to these there is another group who are members of the Church in name, but who have left, and who now in their hearts long to return but do not know how and are too timid to try. They too, in moments of quiet reflection, ask, "Why am I here? Why am I so lost? Please, please help me find my way."

As I think of them I think also of one of the most beautiful stories ever told. May I recount it in the language of Him who first spoke it:

"A certain man had two sons:

"And the younger of them said to his father, Father, give me the portion of goods that falleth to me. And he divided unto them his living.

"And not many days after the younger son gathered all together, and took his journey into a far country, and there wasted his substance with riotous living.

"And when he had spent all, there arose a mighty famine in that land; and he began to be in want.

"And he went and joined himself to a citizen of that country; and he sent him into his fields to feed swine.

"And he would fain have filled his belly with the husks that the swine did eat: and no man gave unto him.

"And when he came to himself, he said, How many hired servants of my father's have bread enough and to spare, and I perish with hunger!

"I will arise and go to my father, and will say unto him, Father, I have sinned against heaven, and before thee,

"And am no more worthy to be called thy son: make me as one of thy hired servants.

"And he arose, and came to his father. But when he was yet a great way off, his father saw him, and had compassion, and ran, and fell on his neck, and kissed him.

"And the son said unto him, Father, I have sinned against heaven, and in thy sight, and am no more worthy to be called thy son.

"But the father said to his servants, Bring forth the best robe, and put it on him; and put his ring on his hand, and shoes on his feet:

"And bring hither the fatted calf, and kill it; and let us eat, and be merry:

"For this my son was dead, and is alive again; he was lost, and is found." (Luke 15:11-24.)

To you who have taken your spiritual inheritance and left, and who now find an emptiness in your lives, the way is open for your return.

Note the words of the parable of the Prodigal Son: "And when he came to himself." Have you not also reflected on your condition and circumstances and longed to return?

The boy in the parable wanted only to be a servant in his father's house, but his father, seeing him afar off, ran to meet him and kissed him, put a robe on his back, a ring on his hand, and shoes on his feet, and had a feast prepared for him.

So it will be with you. If you will take the first timid step to return, you will find open arms to greet you and warm friends to make you welcome.

I think I know why some of you left. You were offended by a thoughtless individual who injured you, and you mistook his actions as representative of the Church. Or you may have moved from an area where you were known to an area where you were largely alone, and grew up there with only little knowledge of the Church. Or you may have been drawn to other company or habits that you felt were incompatible with association in the Church. Or you may have felt yourself wiser in the wisdom of the world than those of your Church associates, and, with some air of disdain, you withdrew yourself from their company.

I am not here to dwell on the reasons. I hope you will not. Put the past behind you. Said the prophet Isaiah in another age, with words that fit our own: "Wash you, make you clean; put away the evil of your doings from before mine eyes; cease to do evil; learn to do well. . . . Come now, and let us reason together, saith the Lord; though your sins be as scarlet, they shall be as white as snow; though they be red like crimson, they shall be as wool. If ye be willing and obedient, ye shall eat the good of the land." (Isaiah 1:16-19.)

This is what the gospel is all about—to make bad men good

and good men better. There is a process of change, a procedure in the Church by which even those who have sinned seriously may come back.

Do not let pride stand in your way. If that is a problem, there is a story from the Old Testament I should like to give you.

Naaman was captain of the host of the king of Syria, a great man, "a mighty man in valour, but he was a leper." And Naaman's wife had a little maid, a daughter of Israel, who said to her mistress: "Would God my Lord [Naaman] were with the prophet that is in Samaria! for he would recover him of his leprosy."

When Naaman heard this, he prepared rich gifts and a letter to the king of Israel. But the king, learning of the reason for Naaman's coming, was frightened, for he had not the power to cleanse the leper. Then Elisha the prophet sent word to the king that he would deal with the captain. "So Naaman came with his horses and with his chariot, and stood at the door of the house of Elisha."

But Elisha did not even so much as go out to greet the captain. He sent a messenger to Naaman, saying, "Go and wash in Jordan seven times, and thy flesh shall come again to thee, and thou shalt be clean."

Naaman was insulted that he should be told to wash in Jordan when there were cleaner streams in his own land, and "he turned and went away in a rage." But his servants pleaded with him to do as Elisha had suggested. The proud captain finally relented, and the scripture records, "Then went he down, and dipped himself seven times in Jordan, according to the saying of the man of God: and his flesh came again like unto the flesh of a little child, and he was clean." (2 Kings 5:1-14.)

And so I repeat, do not let pride stand in your way. The way of the gospel is a simple way. Some of the requirements may appear to you as elementary and unnecessary. Do not spurn them. Humble yourself and walk in obedience. I promise that the results that follow will be marvelous to behold and satisfying to experience.

Where do you begin? How do you get in touch? In every

unit of the Church throughout the world there are two men who have been given responsibility for you. If you do not know them, call the bishop of the ward in which you live, or write a letter to the Church. There will come to you those who can help without embarrassment. In kindness and love and appreciation they will show you the way and take you by the hand and walk with you.

Try it. There is everything to gain and nothing to lose. Come back. There is more of peace to be found in the Church than you have known in a long while. There are many whose friendship you will come to enjoy. There is reading to be done, instruction to be received, discussions in which to participate that will stretch your mind and feed your spirit.

The quiet longings of your heart will be fulfilled. The emptiness you have known for so long will be replaced with a fulness of joy.

I have a friend with whom I served more than forty years ago in the mission field. In the years that followed he went off to war. In his loneliness he picked up with careless companions. He married out of the Church. He followed habits that had made him feel he would not be welcomed. He moved from one part of the country to another. His identity was lost.

One Sunday I found myself in a California city for a stake conference. My name and picture had been in the local newspaper. The phone rang at the stake center as the stake president and I entered the building that morning. The call was for me, and the caller identified himself. He wanted to see me. I excused myself from the meeting I was to have held early that morning and asked the stake president to carry on with it. I had something more important to do.

He came, this friend of mine, timidly and somewhat fearfully. He had been away for a long time. We embraced as brothers long separated. At first the conversation was awkward, but it soon warmed as we discussed together days spent in England many years ago. There were tears in the eyes of this strong man as he spoke of the Church of which he had once been so effective a part, and then told of the long, empty years that had followed. He dwelt upon them as a man speaks of nightmares.

When he had described those wasted years, we talked of his returning. He thought it would be difficult, that it would be embarrassing, but he agreed to try.

I had a letter from him not long ago. He said, "I'm back. I'm back, and how wonderful it feels to be home again."

And so to you who, like him, long to return but are reluctant to take the first step, try. Let us meet you where you now stand, and take you by the hand and help you. I promise you it will feel good to be home again.

I bear you my witness that this is the work of the Lord. It is the kingdom of God in the earth. It bears the name of the Only Begotten of the Father. Here you will find happiness, and strength, and a reassuring peace you have not known for a long while, the peace that passeth all understanding. God bless you to try.

PART II

What We Believe

12

"BE NOT FAITHLESS"

Each spring the Christian world celebrates Easter in remembrance of the resurrection, when the risen Lord appeared first to Mary Magdalene, and later that day to the ten apostles, Thomas being absent.

"The other disciples therefore said unto him, we have seen the Lord." But Thomas, like so many then and now, said, "Except I shall see in his hands the print of the nails, and put my finger into the print of the nails, and thrust my hand into his side, I will not believe." (John 20:25.)

Have you not heard others speak as Thomas spoke? "Give us," they say, "the empirical evidence. Prove before our very eyes, and our ears, and our hands, else we will not believe." This is the language of the time in which we live. Thomas the Doubter has become the example of men in all ages who refuse to accept other than that which they can physically prove and explain—as if they could prove love, or faith, or even such physical phenomena as electricity.

But to continue with the narrative, eight days later the apostles were together again, this time Thomas with them. "Then came Jesus, the doors being shut, and stood in the midst, and said, Peace unto you."

Singling out Thomas, he said: "Reach hither thy finger, and behold my hands; and reach hither thy hand, and thrust it into my side: and *be not faithless, but believing.*"

Thomas, astonished and shaken, answered and said unto him, "My Lord and my God."

Jesus then said to him, "Thomas, because thou hast seen me, thou hast believed: blessed are they that have not seen, and yet have believed." (John 20:26-29. Italics added.)

To all who may have doubts, I repeat the words given Thomas as he felt the wounded hands of the Lord: "Be not faithless, but believing." Believe in Jesus Christ, the Son of God, the greatest figure of time and eternity. Believe that his matchless life reached back before the world was formed. Believe that he was the Creator of the earth on which we live. Believe that he was Jehovah of the Old Testament, that he was the Messiah of the New Testament, that he died and was resurrected, that he visited the western continents and taught the people there, that he ushered in this final gospel dispensation, and that he lives, the living Son of the living God, our Savior and our Redeemer.

John says of the creation that "all things were made by him; and without him was not any thing made that was made." (John 1:3.)

Can anyone who has walked beneath the stars at night, can anyone who has seen the touch of spring upon the land doubt the hand of divinity in creation? So observing the beauties of the earth, one is wont to speak as did the Psalmist: "The heavens declare the glory of God; and the firmament sheweth his handywork. Day unto day uttereth speech, and night unto night sheweth knowledge." (Psalm 19:1-2.)

All beauty in the earth bears the fingerprint of the Master Creator, of those hands which, after they took the form of mortality and then immortality, Thomas insisted on touching before he would believe.

Be not faithless, but believe in Jehovah, he whose finger wrote upon the tablets of stone amid the thunders of Sinai, "Thou shalt have no other gods before me." (Exodus 20:3.) The Decalogue, which is the basis of all good law governing human relations, is the product of his divine genius. As you look upon the vast body of legalisms designed to protect men and society, pause and know that it has its roots in those few brief and timeless declarations given by the all-wise Jehovah to Moses.

Believe in him who was the God of Abraham, Isaac, and Jacob, who was the source of inspiration of all the ancient prophets as they spoke as they were moved upon by the Holy Ghost. They spoke of him when they rebuked kings, when they chastised the nations, and when as seers they looked forward to the coming of a promised Messiah, declaring by the power of revelation, "Therefore the Lord himself shall give you a sign; Behold, a virgin shall conceive, and bear a son, and shall call his name Immanuel." (Isaiah 7:14.)

"And the spirit of the Lord shall rest upon him, the spirit of wisdom and understanding, the spirit of counsel and might, the spirit of knowledge and of the fear of the Lord." (Isaiah 11:2.)

"And the government shall be upon his shoulder: and his name shall be called Wonderful, Counsellor, The mighty God, The everlasting Father, the Prince of Peace." (Isaiah 9:6.)

Doubt not, but believe that it was he who was born to earth in a manger when there was no room in the inn. Well did an angel ask a prophet who had foreseen these things in vision: "Knowest thou the condescension of God?" (1 Nephi 11:16.) I suppose none of us can fully understand that—how the great Jehovah should come among men, his birth in a manger, among a hated people, in a vassal state. But at his birth there was an angelic chorus that sang of his glory. There were shepherds who worshipped him. There was a new star in the east. There were wise men who traveled far to bring tribute of gold, frankincense, and myrrh. One can surmise they touched those tiny hands in wonder and awe as they presented their gifts to the newborn king.

Herod the Great, who knew of the prophecies, feared those hands and sought to destroy them, and in the horrible slaughter of the innocents brought blood upon his own hands and head.

Believe that John the Baptist spoke by the power of revelation when he declared of Jesus, "Behold the Lamb of God, which taketh away the sin of the world." (John 1:29.) And that it was the voice of the Almighty that declared above the waters of Jordan, "This is my beloved Son, in whom I am well pleased." (Matthew 3:17.)

Believe and know that he was a man of miracles. He who had created the world and governed it as the great Jehovah understood the elements of earth and all the functions of life. Beginning at Cana, where he turned the water into wine, he went on to cause the lame to walk, the blind to see, the dead to return to life—he, the Master Physician, who healed the sick by the authority inherent in him as the Son of God.

He was the comforter of the burdened of his time and of all the generations who have come after who have truly believed in him. Said he to each of us: "Come unto me, all ye that labour and are heavy laden, and I will give you rest. Take my yoke upon you, and learn of me; for I am meek and lowly in heart: and ye shall find rest unto your souls. For my yoke is easy, and my burden is light." (Matthew 11:28-30.)

I spoke one day to a friend escaped from his native land. With the fall of his nation, he had been arrested and interned. His wife and children had been able to get away, but for three years and more he had been a prisoner without means of communication with those he loved. The food had been wretched, the living conditions oppressive, with no prospects for improvement.

"What sustained you through all those dark days?" I asked.

He responded: "My faith; my faith in the Lord Jesus Christ. I put my burdens on him, and then they seemed so much the lighter."

On one occasion while the Lord was traveling through Samaria, he wearied and thirsted. Pausing at Jacob's well, he rested and requested a drink from the woman who had come to draw water. In the conversation that followed he declared the saving power of his teaching, saying: "Whosoever drinketh of this water shall thirst again: But whosoever drinketh of the water that I shall give him [it] shall be in him a well of water springing up into everlasting life."

In that same conversation he declared his identity when the woman at the well spoke of the promised Messiah, "which is called Christ." He, without equivocation, said, "I that speak unto thee am he." (John 4:13-14, 25-26.)

Doubt not, but believe that he is the Master of life and

death. To the sorrowing Martha he declared his eternal power, saying: "I am the resurrection, and the life: he that believeth in me, though he were dead, yet shall he live: And whosoever liveth and believeth in me shall never die." (John 11:25-26.)

Were words so great as these ever spoken for the comfort of those who have lost loved ones? Thomas was present when those words were given and also when Lazarus afterwards was called forth from the tomb. Yet he doubted the Lord's power to bring himself forth after the terrible death upon the cross, asserting to his fellow apostles that except he feel the wounds in the hands he would not believe. Small wonder that Jesus rebuked him, saying, "Be not faithless, but believing."

We, like Thomas, are so prone to forget the evidences of his matchless life and power. Those evidences are not found alone in the Bible, the testament of the Old World. There is a testament of the New World which was brought forth by the gift and power of God to the convincing of the Jew and the gentile that Jesus is the Christ. It contains another gospel, beautiful in language and powerful in spirit.

Jesus in his earthly ministry spoke of other sheep of another fold from those he was then teaching and declared that they also should hear his voice, "and there shall be one fold, and one shepherd." (John 10:16.)

At some time following his resurrection a voice was heard from the heavens among a people who were gathered together in the Land Bountiful somewhere on the western continents. It was the voice of God, and it said unto them: "Behold my Beloved Son, in whom I am well pleased, in whom I have glorified my name—hear ye him.

"And . . . they saw a Man descending out of heaven; and he was clothed in a white robe; and he came down and stood in the midst of them," declaring unto them: "Behold, I am Jesus Christ, whom the prophets testified shall come into the world." (3 Nephi 11:7-8, 10.)

He invited them, as he invited Thomas, to feel his hands and side, and they were astonished and cried, "Hosanna! Blessed be the name of the Most High God!" (3 Nephi 11:17.)

They doubted not, but believed, as have millions who have

read this marvelous witness of the resurrected Lord. If there be those who know not of this fifth gospel and desire it, their request will bring it, and it will come with a promise that if they will read prayerfully they shall know of the truth of this remarkable new witness for Christ.

And there is yet another testifier, for as certainly as the voice of God declared the divine Sonship of Jesus at the waters of Jordan, and again on the Mount of Transfiguration, and yet again at the land Bountiful, even so again that same introduction was made in the opening of this gospel dispensation in a glorious vision in which God the Eternal Father and his Son Jesus Christ appeared and spoke to a young man who had come seeking, and who in the years that followed spoke as a prophet of the risen Lord, even giving his life in testimony of him who had died upon the cross.

With so many evidences, and with the conviction borne in our hearts by the power of the Holy Ghost, we add in words of soberness and sincerity and love our testimony of the Lord Jesus Christ; wherefore, O man, "be not faithless, but believing" in him who is the living Son of God, our Savior, our Redeemer.

13

THE MIRACLE
THAT IS JESUS

On the desk in my home I have a small metal box. It is about 12 inches square and half as high. On its face are six knobs and two dials. Now and again, when I have an hour, it becomes my plaything. It is a shortwave radio. Turning the knobs, I listen to London, Washington, Tokyo, Peking, Moscow, Havana, and other great capitals of the world.

The voices I hear are persuasive, seductive, fascinating, and confusing. Speaking across the earth, they are part of a mighty battle that is being waged for the minds of men. They are aimed at persuasion in political philosophy. There are voices of democracy competing with voices of communism, and each is winning converts according to the discernment and the judgment of listeners. The stakes are high, the weapons are sophisticated, the methods are clever.

There is a comparable battle being waged for the faith of men, but the lines are not always so clearly drawn, for even among the forces of Christianity there are those who would destroy the divinity of the Christ in whose name they speak. They might be disregarded if their voices were not so seductive, if their influence were not so far-reaching, if their reasoning were not so subtle.

At sunrise every Easter morning multitudes gather on a

thousand hills to welcome the dawn of the Easter day and to remind themselves of the story of the Christ, whose resurrection they commemorate. In language both beautiful and hopeful, preachers of many faiths recount the story of the empty tomb. To them—and to you—I raise this question: Do you actually believe it?

Do you actually believe that Jesus was the Son of God, the literal offspring of the Father?

Do you believe that the voice of God, the Eternal Father, was heard above the waters of Jordan declaring, "This is my beloved Son, in whom I am well pleased"? (Matthew 3:17.)

Do you believe that this same Jesus was the worker of miracles, the healer of the sick, the restorer of the infirm, the giver of life to the dead?

Do you believe that following his death on Calvary's hill and his burial in Joseph's tomb, he came forth alive the third day?

Do you actually believe that he yet lives—real, vital, and personal—and that he will come again as promised by the angels at his ascension?

Do you actually believe these things? If you do, then you are part of a shrinking body of literalists who more and more are being smiled at by philosophers, who more and more are being ridiculed by certain educators, and who more and more are being considered "out of it" by a growing coterie of ministers of religion and influential theologians.

I once read a series of provocative writings setting forth the clever reasoning of American, British, and European theologians to "demyth," as it is called, the story of Jesus of Nazareth. I quote from a capable Protestant layman who wrote:

"The most disruptive questions are coming from theologians who . . . are questioning every old concept. They even suggest that maybe the word 'God' should be discarded, since it has become meaningless to so many people.

"Stripped of all else, the question the liberal theologians are asking is the old one that has time and again sundered the Christian church: Who was Jesus?

"The revolutionists . . . turn to the Bible as a source of

truth, but their Bible is an expurgated version with embarrassing references to abnormal events edited out. 'De-mythologized,' one says. 'De-literalized,' says another.

"What the new wave casts up is 'religionless' Christianity; a faith grounded on a philosophic system, instead of being suspended precariously from old myths." (*Fortune*, December 1965, p. 173.)

In the eyes of these intellectuals, these are myths—the birth of Jesus as the Son of God of whom the angels sang on Judea's plains, the worker of miracles who healed the sick and raised the dead, the Christ resurrected from the grave, the ascension and the promised return.

These modern theologians strip him of his divinity and then wonder why men do not worship him. These clever scholars have taken from Jesus the mantle of godhood and have left only a man. They have tried to accommodate him to their own narrow thinking. They have robbed him of his divine sonship and taken from the world its rightful King.

While reading of this very effective and growing "de-literalization" process and of its evident effect on the faith of those who are its victims, particularly the youth who are caught up in this sophistry, the words anciently spoken by the prophet Amos come home with new clarity:

"Behold, the days come, saith the Lord God, that I will send a famine in the land, not a famine of bread, nor a thirst for water, but of hearing the words of the Lord: And they shall wander from sea to sea, and from the north even to the east, they shall run to and fro to seek the word of the Lord, and shall not find it. In that day shall the fair virgins and the young men faint for thirst. . . . even they shall fall, and never rise up again." (Amos 8:11-14.)

How descriptive those words are of many of the youth of our day, the young men and the young women who in their hearts hunger for a faith that will satisfy, but who, spurning it because of the manner in which it is offered, "faint for thirst" and "fall, and never rise up again." To these I give solemn witness that God is not dead, except as he is viewed with a lifeless interpretation.

Is a belief in the divinity of our Lord out of date in the twentieth century? The great scientific age of which we are a part does not demand a denial of the miracle that is Jesus. Rather, there was never a time in all the history of man that made more believable that which in the past might have been regarded as supernatural and impossible. How can anyone today regard anything as impossible?

To those acquainted with the giant strides of biological science, where men are beginning to peek into the very nature of life and its creation, the miracle of the birth of Jesus as the Son of God certainly becomes more plausible, even to the doubter.

Further, it is not difficult to believe that he, possessed of knowledge commensurate with the task of creating the earth, could heal the sick, restore the infirm, return the dead to life. It may have been difficult to believe these things in medieval times, but can one reasonably doubt the possibility of such while witnessing the miracles of healing and restoration that occur daily?

Is the ascension so impossible a thing to comprehend after sitting in one's living room and watching the lift-off of a modern spacecraft as it rises into the heavens to seek out with unerring accuracy a companion spaceship orbiting the earth at more than 17,000 miles an hour?

Miracles? I should think so. This is the age of miracles. During my brief lifetime, I have witnessed more of scientific advance than did all of my forebears together during the previous 5,000 years.

With so much of what appears miraculous about me every day, it is easy to believe in the miracle of Jesus.

But a witness of the Lord is not obtained by observation of the accomplishments of men. Such observation makes reasonable a belief in his birth, life, death, and resurrection. But there is needed something more than a reasonable belief. There is needed an understanding of his unique and incomparable position as the divine Redeemer and an enthusiasm for him and his message as the Son of God.

That understanding and that enthusiasm are available to all

who will pay the price. They are not incompatible with higher education, but they will not come of reading philosophy. No, they come of a simpler process. The things of God are understood by the Spirit of God. (1 Corinthians 2:11.) So declares the word of revelation.

The acquisition of understanding and enthusiasm for the Lord comes from following simple rules. I should like to suggest three, elementary in their concept, almost trite in their repetition, but fundamental in their application and fruitful in their result. I suggest them particularly to our young people.

The first is *to read*—to read the word of the Lord. I know that with the demands of your studies there is little time to read anything else. But I promise you that if you will read the words of that writing which we call scripture, there will come into your heart an understanding and a warmth that will be pleasing to experience. "Search the scriptures; for in them ye think ye have eternal life: and they are they which testify of me." (John 5:39.) Read, for instance, the Gospel of John from its beginning to its end. Let the Lord speak for himself to you, and his words will come with a quiet conviction that will make the words of his critics meaningless. Read also the testament of the New World, the Book of Mormon, brought forth as a witness "that Jesus is the Christ, the Eternal God, manifesting himself unto all nations." (Book of Mormon title page.)

The next is *to serve*—to serve in the work of the Lord. Spiritual strength is like physical strength; it is like the muscle of my arm. It grows only as it is nourished and exercised.

The cause of Christ does not need your doubts; it needs your strength and time and talents, and as you exercise these in service, your faith will grow and your doubts will wane.

The Lord declared: "He that findeth his life shall lose it: and he that loseth his life for my sake shall find it." (Matthew 10:39.) These words have something more than a cold theological meaning. They are a statement of a law of life—that as we lose ourselves in a great cause we find ourselves—and there is no greater cause than that of the Master.

The third is *to pray*. Speak with your Eternal Father in the name of his Beloved Son. "Behold," he says, "I stand at the door, and knock; if any man hear my voice, and open the door, I will come in to him, and will sup with him, and he with me." (Revelation 3:20.)

This is his invitation, and the promise is sure. It is unlikely that you will hear voices from heaven, but there will come a heaven-sent assurance, peaceful and certain.

In that great conversation between Jesus and Nicodemus, the Lord declared: "That which is born of the flesh is flesh; and that which is born of the Spirit is spirit." Then he went on to say, "The wind bloweth where it listeth, and thou hearest the sound thereof, but canst not tell whence it cometh, and whither it goeth: so is every one that is born of the Spirit." (John 3:6, 8.)

I do not hesitate to promise that it will be so with you. If you will read the word of the Lord, if you will serve in his cause, if in prayer you will talk with him, your doubts will leave; and shining through all of the confusion of philosophy, so-called higher criticism, and negative theology will come the witness of the Holy Spirit that Jesus is in very deed the Son of God, born in the flesh, the Redeemer of the world resurrected from the grave, the Lord who shall come to reign as King of kings. It is your opportunity so to know. It is your obligation so to find out. God bless you so to do.

14

THE SYMBOL
OF CHRIST

Following a complete renovation of the Arizona Temple at Mesa, nearly a quarter of a million people saw its beautiful interior. On the first day of the opening, clergymen of other religions were invited as special guests, and hundreds responded. It was my privilege to speak to them and to answer their questions at the conclusion of their tours. I told them that we would be pleased to answer any queries they might have. Many were asked. Among these was one that came from a Protestant minister.

Said he: "I've been all through this building, this temple which carries on its face the name of Jesus Christ, but nowhere have I seen any representation of the cross, the symbol of Christianity. I have noted your buildings elsewhere and likewise find an absence of the cross. Why is this, when you say you believe in Jesus Christ?"

I responded: "I do not wish to give offense to any of my Christian brethren who use the cross on the steeples of their cathedrals and at the altars of their chapels, who wear it on their vestments, and imprint it on their books and other literature. But for us, the cross is the symbol of the dying Christ, while our message is a declaration of the living Christ."

He then asked: "If you do not use the cross, what is the symbol of your religion?"

I replied that the lives of our people must become the only meaningful expression of our faith and in fact, therefore, the symbol of our worship.

I hope he did not feel that I was smug or self-righteous in my response. He was correct in his observation that we do not use the cross, except as our military chaplains use it on their uniforms for identification. Our position at first glance may seem a contradiction of our profession that Jesus Christ is the key figure of our faith. The official name of the church is The Church of Jesus Christ of Latter-day Saints. We worship him as Lord and Savior. The Bible is our scripture. We believe that the prophets of the Old Testament who foretold the coming of the Messiah spoke under divine inspiration. We glory in the accounts of Matthew, Mark, Luke, and John, setting forth the events of the birth, ministry, death, and resurrection of the Son of God, the Only Begotten of the Father in the flesh. Like Paul of old, we are "not ashamed of the gospel of [Jesus] Christ: for it is the power of God unto salvation." (Romans 1:16.) And like Peter, we affirm that Jesus Christ is the only name "given among men, whereby we must be saved." (Acts 4:12.)

The Book of Mormon, which we regard as the testament of the New World, setting forth the teachings of prophets who lived anciently in the Western Hemisphere, testifies of him who was born in Bethlehem of Judea and who died on the hill of Calvary. To a world wavering in its faith, it is another and powerful witness of the divinity of the Lord. Its very preface, written by a prophet who walked the Americas a millennium and a half ago, categorically states that it was written "to the convincing of the Jew and Gentile that JESUS is the CHRIST, the ETERNAL GOD, manifesting himself unto all nations."

And in our book of modern revelation, the Doctrine and Covenants, he has declared himself in these certain words: "I am Alpha and Omega, Christ the Lord; yea, even I am he, the beginning and the end, the Redeemer of the world." (D&C 19:1.)

In light of such declarations, in view of such testimony, well might many ask, as my minister friend in Arizona asked, if you profess a belief in Jesus Christ, why do you not use the symbol of his death, the cross of Calvary?

To this I must first reply that no member of the Church must ever forget the terrible price paid by our Redeemer who gave his life that all men might live—the agony of Gethsemane, the bitter mockery of his trial, the vicious crown of thorns tearing at his flesh, the blood cry of the mob before Pilate, the lonely burden of his heavy walk along the way to Calvary, the terrifying pain as great nails pierced his hands and feet, the fevered torture of his body as he hung that tragic day, the Son of God crying out, "Father, forgive them; for they know not what they do." (Luke 23:34.)

This was the cross, the instrument of his torture, the terrible device designed to destroy the Man of Peace, the evil recompense for his miraculous work of healing the sick, of causing the blind to see, of raising the dead. This was the cross on which he hung and died on Golgotha's lonely summit.

We cannot forget that. We must never forget it, for here our Savior, our Redeemer, the Son of God, gave himself a vicarious sacrifice for each of us. But the gloom of that dark evening before the Jewish Sabbath, when his lifeless body was taken down and hurriedly laid in a borrowed tomb, drained away the hope of even his most ardent and knowing disciples. They were bereft, not understanding what he had told them earlier. Dead was the Messiah in whom they believed. Gone was their Master in whom they had placed all of their longing, their faith, their hope. He who had spoken of everlasting life, he who had raised Lazarus from the grave, now had died as surely as all men before him had died. Now had come the end to his sorrowful, brief life. That life had been as Isaiah had long before foretold: He was "despised and rejected of men; a man of sorrows, and acquainted with grief. . . . He was wounded for our transgressions, he was bruised for our iniquities: the chastisement of our peace was upon him." (Isaiah 53:3, 5.) Now he was gone.

We can only speculate on the feelings of those who loved him as they pondered his death during the long hours of the Jewish Sabbath, the Saturday of our calendar.

Then dawned the first day of the week, the Sabbath of the Lord as we have come to know it. To those who came to the tomb, heavy with sorrow, an attending angel declared, "Why seek ye the living among the dead? He is not here. . . . he is risen, as he said." (Matthew 28:6.)

Here was the greatest miracle of human history. Earlier he had told them, "I am the resurrection and the life." (John 11:25.) But they had not understood. Now they knew. He had died in misery and pain and loneliness. Now, on the third day, he arose in power and beauty and life, the first fruits of all who slept, the assurance for men of all ages that "as in Adam all die, even so in Christ shall all be made alive." (1 Corinthians 15:22.)

On Calvary he was the dying Jesus. From the tomb he emerged the living Christ. The cross had been the bitter fruit of Judas's betrayal, the summary of Peter's denial. The empty tomb now became the testimony of His divinity, the assurance of eternal life, the answer to Job's unanswered question: "If a man die, shall he live again?" (Job 14:14.)

Having died, he might have been forgotten, or, at best, remembered as one of many great teachers whose lives are epitomized in a few lines in the books of history. Now, having been resurrected, he became the Master of Life. Now, with Isaiah, his disciples could sing with certain faith: "His name shall be called Wonderful, Counseller, The mighty God, The everlasting Father, The Prince of Peace." (Isaiah 9:6.)

Fulfilled were the expectant words of Job: "For I know that my redeemer liveth, and that he shall stand at the latter-day upon the earth: And though after my skin worms destroy this body, yet in my flesh shall I see God: Whom I shall see for myself, and mine eyes shall behold, and not another; though my reins be consumed within me." (Job 19:25-27.)

Well did Mary cry, "Rabboni!" (John 20:16) when first she saw the risen Lord, for master now he was in very deed, master not only of life, but of death itself. Gone was the sting of death, broken the victory of the grave.

The fearful Peter was transformed. Even the doubtful Thomas declared in soberness and reverence and realism, "My Lord and my God!" (John 20:28.) "Be not faithless, but believing" (John 20:27) were the unforgettable words of the Lord on that marvelous occasion.

There followed appearances to many, including, as Paul records, "above five hundred brethren at once." (1 Corinthians 15:6.)

And in the Western Hemisphere were other sheep of whom he had spoken earlier. The people there "heard a voice as if it came out of heaven . . . and it said unto them: Behold my Beloved Son, in whom I am well pleased, in whom I have glorified my name—hear ye him.

". . . And behold, they saw a Man descending out of heaven; and he was clothed in a white robe; and he came down and stood in the midst of them. . . .

"And it came to pass that he stretched forth his hand and spake unto the people, saying: Behold, I am Jesus Christ, whom the prophets testified [should] come into the world. . . . Arise and come forth unto me." (3 Nephi 11:3, 6, 8-10, 14.)

And now finally there are modern witnesses, for he came again to open this dispensation, the dispensation of the prophesied fulness of times. In a glorious vision, he—the resurrected, living Lord—and his Father, the God of heaven, appeared to a boy prophet to begin anew the restoration of ancient truth. There followed a veritable "cloud of witnesses" (Hebrews 12:1), and he who had been the recipient—Joseph Smith, the modern prophet—declared with words of soberness:

"And now, after the many testimonies which have been given of him, this is the testimony, last of all, which we give of him: That he lives!

"For we saw him, even on the right hand of God; and we heard the voice bearing record that he is the Only Begotten of the Father—

"That by him, and through him, and of him, the worlds are and were created, and the inhabitants thereof are begotten sons and daughters unto God." (D&C 76:22-24.)

To this may be added the witness of millions who, by the power of the Holy Spirit, have borne and now bear solemn testimony of his living reality. That testimony has been their comfort and their strength.

For instance, I have been thinking much of late of a friend

in Vietnam. I know not where he is or what his condition may be. I know only that he is a man of quiet and transcendent faith in God, our Eternal Father, and in his Son, the living Christ. As the light of freedom has flickered and died in that land of sorrow, I think I can hear him sing, as I have heard him sing before,

> When through the deep waters I call thee to go,
> The rivers of sorrow shall not thee o'erflow;
> For I will be with thee, thy troubles to bless,
> And sanctify to thee thy deepest distress.
> —Hymns, no. 66

And so, because our Savior lives, we do not use the symbol of his death as the symbol of our faith. But what shall we use? No sign, no work of art, no representation of form is adequate to express the glory and the wonder of the living Christ. He told us what that symbol should be when he said, "If ye love me, keep my commandments." (John 14:15.)

As his followers, we cannot do a mean or shoddy or ungracious thing without tarnishing his image. Nor can we do a good and gracious and generous act without burnishing more brightly the symbol of him whose name we have taken upon ourselves.

And so our lives must become a meaningful expression, the symbol of our declaration of our testimony of the living Christ, the Eternal Son of the living God.

It is that simple and that profound and we'd better never forget it.

> I know that my Redeemer lives—
> Triumphant Savior, Son of God,
> Victorious over pain and death,
> My King, my Leader, and my Lord.
>
> He lives, my one sure rock of faith,
> The one bright hope of men on earth,
> The beacon to a better way,
> The light beyond the veil of death.

THE SYMBOL OF CHRIST

O give me Thy sweet spirit still,
The peace that comes alone from Thee,
The faith to walk the lonely road
That leads to Thine eternity.

15

"THE HEAVENS ARE NOT STAYED"

We believe all that God has revealed, all that He does now reveal, and we believe that He will yet reveal many great and important things pertaining to the Kingdom of God." (Article of Faith 9.)

This statement from the Prophet Joseph Smith is the creed, the guide, the foundation of the faith of all members of The Church of Jesus Christ of Latter-day Saints.

God is the one sure source of truth. He is the fount of all inspiration. It is from him that the world must receive direction if peace is to come to the earth and if goodwill is to prevail among men. This earth is his creation. We are his children. Out of the love he bears for us, he will guide us if we will seek, listen, and obey. "Surely the Lord God will do nothing, but he revealeth his secrets unto his servants the prophets." (Amos 3:7.)

Our world is changing. We live in an age of great material progress. Can religion remain static when all else is moving forward?

It is true that man's essential nature does not change, and that principles laid down centuries ago by the prophets are as applicable today as they were when they were first enunciated; but the world evidently knows not how to apply them. Today that application needs the direction of the Almighty as certainly as when Jehovah spoke to Enoch and Moses and Isaiah and Elijah.

"For the prophecy came not in old time by the will of man: but holy men of God spake as they were moved by the Holy Ghost." (2 Peter 1:21.) And prophecy, which is revelation, comes not now, nor will it come in the future, by the will of man, but only as men of God speak as they are moved upon by that same spirit.

How poverty-ridden is our world in the wisdom of living one with another. The stresses, the strains, the tensions in human relationships, the wars and rumors of wars that constantly afflict us all become evidence that "the wisdom of their wise men shall perish, and the understanding of their prudent men shall be hid." (Isaiah 29:14.) Religion, to be effective, must be a vital and timely force in the lives of men.

The people today need a prophet as surely as Israel needed a prophet when it groaned in the toils of Egypt, and Moses was called to lead it from bondage.

Israel today has a prophet, and we give our witness to the world that the channel of communication is open between God and his appointed servant.

We would not take from men of good will anywhere the standards of truth by which they live. But we say to all, "Come, feast upon that which the Lord has offered in our day. To that which you have and cherish, we invite you to add that which your Father has further offered, for there is a prophet in the land today as certainly as there was in ancient Israel."

There are those who have declared that the canon of scripture is full, that revelation ceased with the ancient apostles, that the heavens are sealed. Well might we ask such, "Why, then, do you pray? If God is unwilling to speak, is unwilling to guide, if there can be no revelation, why seek him?" The fallacy of this position is evident; yet the world would deny the possibility of modern revelation.

Several years ago I had the opportunity of participating in the opening of our mission in the Philippines. It was an inspirational experience. We gathered at dawn in the American military cemetery on the outskirts of the city of Manila. There before us stood "row on row" the crosses that mark the graves of more than 17,000 American dead, and inscribed on marble tablets we saw the name of some 36,000 more who died in the battles of the Pacific and whose remains were never found—a grim and solemn reminder of man's foolish inhumanity to man.

Among those who spoke on that sacred occasion was a young Filipino. He recounted the story of how, when he was a child, he had found an old magazine in a pile of trash. It contained an article on the history of our people. It spoke of Joseph Smith. It described him as a prophet. That word *prophet* caught in his consciousness. It impressed him. It raised questions in his young mind. "Could there really be a prophet in the earth in this time of the world?" he asked himself.

Years passed. There came to his land the terrible tragedies of Corregidor and Bataan and the death march to Tarlac; the strafing and bombing of Clark Field near his home; the hunger and fear and oppression of the enemy occupation; and then, finally, the liberation of the Philippines and the reestablishment of Clark Field as an American air base. He secured employment there. One day he heard that one of the American officers for whom he worked was a Mormon. There flashed again into his mind the word *prophet*. He found courage to ask the man if a prophet really stood at the head of his church. Without equivocation the officer replied yes, and there followed an explanation, a recounting of the simple and beautiful story of the appearance of God the Eternal Father and his Son, the Lord Jesus Christ, to a boy who had come in faith and prayer to find wisdom. That testimony touched this young Filipino's heart. His life had been changed by the conviction that revelation from God is available to man in our time. Today he holds the priesthood and walks in the dignity of that priesthood, a leader of the Church in his own land.

Can one doubt the need for revelation in this day of complex human problems? A few years ago news was broadcast over the country that at a particular hour on a particular day the surgeon general of the United States would issue a report on the effects of smoking. The release time was carefully planned, presumably to affect the stock market least seriously. Then, at the appointed hour, radio, television, and the news services dramatically announced the finding of causal relationships between the smoking of cigarets and lung cancer. Lengthy tables of statistics, page upon page of data, were enumerated to produce the conclusion that cigaret smoking is harmful to health. I thumbed through that 387-page report, and then I turned to the revelation of the Lord given through the Prophet Joseph Smith wherein he said simply but unequivocally, "Tobacco . . . is not good for man." (D&C 89:8.)

I am grateful for the work of those scientists who made the report on smoking. I am confident that their discoveries have saved untold suffering and added untold years of useful living to those who heed their counsel. But how much suffering, how many deaths upon which their conclusions were based, might have been avoided had those who became statistics for a government report listened to the word of revelation given by a prophet of God.

As I reflected on that situation—the months of research by able men of science, the vast calculations of electronic computers, the great fanfare of announcements, the background stories, the editorials, the debates, all of this and more, in contrast with the simple, revealed word of the Lord—there came to mind the experience of Elijah on Mount Horeb: ". . . and a great and strong wind rent the mountains, and brake in pieces the rocks before the Lord; but the Lord was not in the wind: and after the wind an earthquake; but the Lord was not in the earthquake: And after the earthquake a fire; but the Lord was not in the fire: and after the fire a still small voice." (1 Kings 19:11-12.)

Such almost invariably has been the word of God as it has come to us, not with trumpets, not from the council halls of the learned, but in the still small voice of revelation. Listening to those who seek in vain to find wisdom and who declaim loudly their nostrums for the ills of the world, one is prone to reply with the Psalmist, "Be still, and know that I am God" (Psalm 46:10), and with the Savior, "He that hath ears to hear, let him hear" (Matthew 11:15).

I wish to make it clear that I do not disparage education, research, study, counsel. I believe most strongly in these. But I believe even more that this troubled world would do well to listen to the source of all true wisdom, to accept all that God

95

has revealed, all that he does now reveal, and to believe that he will yet reveal many great and important things.

Let it be remembered that "the things of God are understood by the Spirit of God," and that revelation is fruitless unless it be listened to and obeyed.

We have a simple and marvelous hymn among us. It came from the pen of an English convert, an orphan boy, a man of Sheffield, a cutler in the steel mills, who more than a century ago wrote out of the testimony of his soul this great song of gratitude, "We thank thee, O God, for a prophet to guide us in these latter days."

To the world we give our witness that there is revelation of the word of God as certainly in the atomic age as there was in the age of Jeremiah. It is just that simple and just that true.

Joseph Smith was the anointed of the Lord to this dispensation. Well might we repeat the words of the Lord: "What power shall stay the heavens? As well might man stretch forth his puny arm to stop the Missouri river in its decreed course, or to turn it up stream, as to hinder the Almighty from pouring down knowledge from heaven upon the heads of the Latter-day Saints." (D&C 121:33.) Knowledge has been and is being revealed. Those who accept it and obey it find that peace which passeth understanding and that growth which leads to eternal life. As surely as Joseph was a prophet, so also are his successors in office, each of those inspired men whom we have sustained and now sustain as prophets, seers, and revelators of the Church.

God help us to be obedient to their counsel.

16

"AN ANGEL FROM ON HIGH"

We often sing in our congregations a favorite hymn, the words of which were written well over a century ago by Parley P. Pratt. He wrote:

> An angel from on high
> The long, long silence broke,
> Descending from the sky,
> These gracious words he spoke:
> "Lo in Cumorah's lonely hill,
> A sacred record lies concealed."
>
> Sealed by Moroni's hand,
> It has for ages lain
> To wait the Lord's command
> From dust to speak again.
> It shall again to light come forth
> To usher in Christ's reign on earth.
>
> It speaks of Joseph's seed
> And makes the remnant known
> Of nations long since dead,
> Who once had dwelt alone.
> The fulness of the gospel, too,
> Its pages will reveal to view.
>
> —Hymns, no. 224

These words represent Parley P. Pratt's declaration of the miraculous coming forth of a remarkable book. That book was first set in type and printed in Palmyra, New York, in the spring of 1830.

Permit me to tell you how Parley Pratt came to know of the book about which he wrote these words. In August of 1830, as a lay preacher, he was traveling from Ohio to eastern New York. At Newark, along the Erie Canal, he left the boat and walked ten miles into the country where he met a Baptist deacon by the name of Hamlin, who told him "of a *book*, a STRANGE BOOK, a VERY STRANGE BOOK! . . . This book, he said, purported to have been originally written on plates either of gold or brass, by a branch of the tribes of Israel; and to have been discovered and translated by a young man near Palmyra, in the State of New York, by the aid of visions, or the ministry of angels. I inquired of him how or where the book was to be obtained. He promised me the perusal of it, at his house the next day. . . . . Next morning I called at his house, where, for the first time, my eyes beheld the 'BOOK OF MORMON'—that book of books . . . which was the principal means, in the hands of God, of directing the entire course of my future life.

"I opened it with eagerness, and read its title page. I then read the testimony of several witnesses in relation to the manner of its being found and translated. After this I commenced its contents by course. I read all day; eating was a burden, I had no desire for food; sleep was a burden when the night came, for I preferred reading to sleep.

"As I read, the spirit of the Lord was upon me, and I knew and comprehended that the book was true, as plainly and manifestly as a man comprehends and knows that he exists." (*Autobiography of Parley P. Pratt* [Deseret Book Co., 1938], pp. 36-37.)

Parley Pratt was then twenty-three years of age. The reading of the Book of Mormon affected him so profoundly that he was soon baptized into the Church and became one of its most effective and powerful advocates. In the course of his ministry he traveled from coast to coast across what is now the United States, into Canada, and to England; he opened the work in the isles of the Pacific and was the first Mormon elder to set foot on the soil of South America. In 1857, while serving a mission in Arkansas, he was shot in the back and killed by an assailant. He was buried in a rural area near the community of Alma, and today in that quiet place a large block of polished granite marks the site of his grave. Incised in its surface are the words of another of his great and prophetic hymns, setting forth his vision of the work in which he was engaged:

> The morning breaks; the shadows flee;
> Lo, Zion's standard is unfurled! . . .
> The dawning of a brighter day
> Majestic rises on the world.
>
> The clouds of error disappear
> Before the rays of truth divine; . . .
> The glory bursting from afar
> Wide o'er the nations soon will shine.
> —Hymns, no. 269

Parley Pratt's experience with the Book of Mormon was not unique. As the volumes of the first edition were circulated and read, strong men and women by the hundreds were so deeply touched that they gave up everything they owned, and in the years that followed not a few even gave their lives for the witness they carried in their hearts of the truth of this remarkable volume.

Today, more than a century and a half after its first publication, it is more widely read than at any time in its history. Whereas there were 5,000 copies in that first edition, today's editions are ordered in lots of as many as a million, and the book currently is printed in more than a score of languages.

Its appeal is as timeless as truth, as universal as mankind. It is the only book that contains within its covers a promise that by divine power the reader may know with certainty of its truth.

Its origin is miraculous; when the story of that origin is first told to one unfamiliar with it, it is almost unbelievable. But the book is here to be felt and handled and read. No one can dispute its presence. All efforts to account for its origin, other than the account given by Joseph Smith, have been shown to lack substance. It is a record of ancient America. It is a scripture of the New World, as certainly as the Bible is the scripture of the Old. Each speaks of the other. Each carries with it the spirit of inspiration, the power to convince and to convert. Together they become two witnesses, hand in hand, that Jesus is the Christ, the resurrected and living Son of the living God.

Its narrative is a chronicle of nations long since gone. But in its descriptions of the problems of today's society, it is as current as the morning newspaper and much more definitive, inspired, and inspiring concerning the solutions of those problems.

I know of no other writing that sets forth with such clarity the tragic consequences to societies that follow courses contrary to the commandments of God. Its pages trace the stories of two distinct civilizations that flourished on this Western Hemisphere. Each began as a small nation, its people walking in the fear of the Lord. But with prosperity came growing evils. The people succumbed to the wiles of the ambitious and scheming leaders who oppressed them with burdensome taxes, who lulled them with hollow promises, who countenanced and even encouraged loose and lascivious living, who led them into terrible wars that resulted in the deaths of millions and the final and total extinction of two great civilizations in two different eras.

No other written testament so clearly illustrates the fact that when men and nations walk in the fear of God and in obedience to his commandments, they prosper and grow, but when they disregard him and his word, there comes a decay that, unless arrested by righteousness, leads to impotence and death. The Book of Mormon is an affirmation of the Old Testament proverb, "Righteousness exalteth a nation: but sin is a reproach to any people." (Proverbs 14:34.)

Those of us in the good land of America are now hearing much debate concerning the treaty designed to reduce the likelihood of nuclear attack on this continent. There is much talk of a balance of power and of a balance of terror. In the context of this current discussion I should like to point out what the God of heaven said long ago concerning this land as recorded in the book of which we are speaking: "Behold, this is a choice land, and whatsoever nation shall possess it shall be free from bondage, and from captivity, and from all other nations under heaven, if they will but serve the God of the land, who is Jesus Christ." (Ether 2:12.)

While this book speaks with power to the issues that affect our modern society, the great and stirring burden of its message is a testimony, vibrant and true, that Jesus is the Christ, the promised Messiah, he who walked the dusty roads of Palestine healing the sick and teaching the doctrines of salvation; who died upon the cross of Calvary; who on the third day came forth from the tomb, appearing to many; and who, prior to his final ascension, visited the people of the Western Hemisphere, concerning whom he earlier had said: "And other sheep I have, which are not of this fold: them also I must bring, and they shall hear my voice; and there shall be one fold, and one shepherd." (John 10:16.)

For centuries the Bible stood alone as a written testimony of the divinity of Jesus of Nazareth. Now, at its side, stands a second and powerful witness that has come forth "to the convincing of the Jew and Gentile that Jesus is the Christ, the Redeemer of the world." (Book of Mormon title page.)

I should like to make a request and offer a challenge to members of the Church throughout the world and to our friends everywhere to read the Book of Mormon. Then I should like to challenge each one to put to the test the words of the prophet Moroni, written as he completed his record fifteen centuries ago. Said he:

"And I exhort you to remember these things; for the time speedily cometh that ye shall know that I lie not, for ye shall see me at the bar of God; and the Lord God will say unto you: Did I not declare my words unto you, which were written by this man, like as one crying from the dead, yea, even as one speaking out of the dust?

"And God shall show unto you, that that which I have written is true." (Moroni 10:27, 29.)

Without reservation I promise you that if you will read the Book of Mormon, there will come into your life and into your home an added measure of the Spirit of the Lord, a strengthened resolution to walk in obedience to his commandments, and a stronger testimony of the living reality of the Son of God.

17

THE STICK OF JOSEPH

I heard on one occasion an officer of the Air Force stand before a group and tell of the circumstances surrounding his coming into the Church. He said in substance: "I had a date with a lovely young woman. When I called for her, I noticed on the table a copy of the Book of Mormon. I had never heard of it before. I began to read. I became interested. I secured a copy of the book and read it through. I had only the traditional idea of God and Jesus Christ. I had never given serious thought to the matter. But as I read this book there came into my mind light and understanding of eternal truths, and into my heart a testimony that God is our Eternal Father, and that Jesus is our Savior."

I am confident that the experience of this man who was influenced by the Book of Mormon is similar to that of many others of our people. If there are miracles among us, certainly one of them is this book. Unbelievers may doubt the First Vision and say there were not witnesses to prove it. Critics may scorn every divine manifestation incident to the coming forth of this work as being of such an intangible nature as to be unprovable to the pragmatic mind, as if the things of God could be understood other than by the Spirit of God. They may discount our theology. But they cannot in honesty dismiss the Book of Mormon. It is here. They can feel it. They can read it. They can weigh its substance and its content. They can witness its influence.

Faced with its presence, but unwilling to believe the story of its coming forth, they have sought an explanation for it, other than the one given by the Prophet that it was engraven on golden plates by ancient prophet-historians, and that their record was revealed and translated by the gift and power of God.

While its detractors have called it blasphemous, the work of a paranoiac, the outpouring of a myth-maker, the result of a man's environment, the Book of Mormon has gone forth to change for good the lives of men and women in many nations. What a concourse of the people of the earth we would have if all of those who have read this book and been influenced by its message were gathered together in one place.

The same book that converted Brigham Young, Willard Richards, Orson and Parley Pratt, and many others of the early leaders of the Church is also converting people in Germany, in the British Isles, in Finland, in Japan, in Tonga, and wherever else men and women are reading it prayerfully and with real intent. The promise of Moroni, written in his loneliness following the destruction of his people, is being fulfilled every day.

Each time we encourage a man to read the Book of Mormon we do him a favor. If he reads it prayerfully and with a sincere desire to know the truth, he will know by the power of the Holy Ghost that the book is true. And from that knowledge there will flow a conviction of the truth of many other things.

For if the Book of Mormon is true, then God lives. Testimony upon testimony runs through its pages of the solemn fact that our Father is real, that he is personal, that he loves his children and seeks their happiness.

If the Book of Mormon is true, then Jesus is the Son of God, the Only Begotten of the Father in the flesh, born of Mary, "a virgin most beautiful above all other virgins," for the book so testifies in a description unexcelled in all literature.

If the Book of Mormon is true, then Jesus is verily our Redeemer, the Savior of the world.

If the Book of Mormon is true, then this land is choice above all other lands; but if it is to remain such, the inhabitants of the land must worship the God of the land, the Lord Jesus

Christ. The histories of two great nations, told with warning in this sacred volume, indicate that while we must have science, while we must have education, while we must have arms, we must also have righteousness if we are to merit the protection of God.

If the Book of Mormon is true, Joseph Smith was a prophet of God, for he was the instrument in the hands of God in bringing to light this testimony of the divinity of our Lord.

If this book is true, Spencer W. Kimball is a prophet, for he holds all the keys, the gifts, powers, and authority held by the Prophet Joseph who brought forth this latter-day work.

I repeat, if the Book of Mormon is true, the Church is true, for the same authority under which this sacred record came to light is present and manifest among us today. It is a restoration of the Church set up by the Savior in Palestine. It is a restoration of the Church set up by the Savior when he visited this continent as set forth in this sacred record.

If the Book of Mormon is true, the Bible is true. The Bible is the Testament of the Old World. The Book of Mormon is the Testament of the New. The one is the record of Judah, the other is the record of Joseph, and they have come together in the hand of the Lord in fulfillment of the prophecy of Ezekiel. Together they declare the Kingship of the Redeemer of the world, and the reality of his kingdom.

Here is a voice that has spoken from the dust with a familiar spirit and touched the hearts of men and women in many lands. Those who have read it prayerfully, be they rich or poor, learned or unlearned, have grown under its power.

Let me tell you of a letter we received a few years ago. A man wrote saying in substance: "I am in a federal reformatory in Ohio. I recently came across a copy of the Book of Mormon in the prison library. I have read it, and when I read Mormon's lamentation over his fallen people—'O ye fair ones, how could ye have departed from the ways of the Lord, how could ye have rejected that Jesus, who stood with open arms to receive you! Behold, if ye had not done this, ye would not have fallen . . .' (Mormon 6:17-18)—when I read this I felt that Mormon was talking to me. Can I get a copy of that book?"

We sent him a copy. He walked in the office some months

later, a changed man. I am happy to report that a young man who had stolen gasoline, and then stolen automobiles, and then done other things until finally he was placed in a federal reformatory, was touched by the spirit of this book, and the report today is that he is now a successful man, rehabilitated, earning a living honestly for himself and family.

Such has been the power of this great book in the lives of those who have read it prayerfully. I give you my testimony that it is true. That I know by the witness of the Holy Ghost, and that knowledge to me is certain.

Sidney Rigdon did not write it. Oliver Cowdery did not write it. It is not the result of a paranoiac or of a dissociated personality, as some have said. It is not the product of a myth-maker. It is not the result of the environment of a farm boy who grew up in western New York. Joseph Smith did not write it. He, the prophet of this dispensation, translated the writings of prophets of old under the power of God, to testify in our day.

We invite all persons everywhere to read it. Its witness lies within itself.

18

A PERSONAL VIEW

OF OUR HISTORY

The soil that Peter Whitmer and his sons cultivated in 1830 in New York State is still farmed and is still productive. The immediate area remains essentially rural, the roads narrow, the houses scattered. The old home of the Whitmer family has been authentically restored—the walls, floors, and roof structure formed of logs from buildings that were erected in the area prior to 1830. Archaeological research, locating the old stone footings, determined the precise location and size—twenty feet by thirty feet. It contained two rooms on the main floor, with two more in the loft above. A substantial rock fireplace provided warmth against the bitter New York winters. All of this has been recreated in a most careful manner to restore what was previously there.

The log house is part of a three-building complex. Directly opposite is the newer farmhouse, constructed years later, more commodious and ornate, its Doric columns affording a look of dignity. Between the two homes is an impressively beautiful new meetinghouse, architecturally faithful to the 1830 period, its gleaming white wood siding and mullioned windows giving the flavor of colonial New England, and its gold dome speaking of the Greek Revival architecture followed in western New York, as seen in the old courthouse in nearby Canandaigua.

The building houses a small and quiet chapel, the woodwork of which represents the very best of the millwright's art. Two wings lead off from the chapel, the one housing class-rooms, the other a visitors center. This has been provided to accommodate those who will come by the many thousands from over the earth, to stand where Joseph stood that historic April 6, 1830, when the Church was organized.

Now, a century and a half after the day of organization, one can in imagination return to that historic Tuesday which had been designated by revelation as the day to organize anew the Church of Jesus Christ.

Peter Whitmer, Sr., had offered the use of his home for the organization meeting just as he had proffered its use a year earli-er to Joseph Smith and Oliver Cowdery for the work of translat-ing the sacred record that became the Book of Mormon.

Now, on the appointed day of April 6, there gathered a sub-stantial number at the Whitmer farm. Some had previously been baptized; some had not. One can envision the horses tied to the fence, their saddles draped over the rails, and the wagons and buggies parked about the yard, with the harnesses thrown on the seats. Those who had gathered from far and near expect-ed to be there for some hours. This was an occasion they had looked forward to with much expectancy. At least thirty men and women, and perhaps as many as sixty, crowded into the small house. The proceedings were simple. Joseph Smith, then twenty-four years of age, called the meeting to order and desig-nated five of his associates to join with him as the actual incor-porators to meet the legal requirement in forming a religious so-ciety.

Those present knelt in solemn prayer. Joseph then asked if they were willing to accept him and Oliver as their teachers and spiritual advisers. All assented to this, thereby instituting oper-ation of the principle of common consent which has subse-quently been followed in the naming of all Church officers. Following this, Joseph ordained Oliver an elder, and Oliver in turn ordained Joseph. The sacrament of the Lord's Supper was administered, the prayers used in this ordinance having been given through revelation. (See D&C 20:75-79.)

Joseph and Oliver then laid their hands upon the heads of

those who had been baptized, confirming them members of the Church and bestowing upon them the gift of the Holy Ghost. Next, some of the men were ordained to various offices in the priesthood. Through revelation received on this occasion, Joseph was designated "a seer, a translator, a prophet, an apostle of Jesus Christ." (D&C 21:1.) Speaking in this capacity of authority, he instructed those present on how to build up the Church and exhorted them "to be faithfull in all things," declaring that "this is the work of God." (Joseph Knight, Sr., "Manuscript of the Early History of Joseph Smith Finding of Plates, &c. &c.," Archives of The Church of Jesus Christ of Latter-day Saints, Salt Lake City, p. 7.) Following the meeting, others were baptized, including Joseph's father and mother and his friend Martin Harris.

Thus, under those simple circumstances, was established in these latter days the Church of Jesus Christ, "built upon the foundation of the apostles and prophets, Jesus Christ himself being the chief corner stone," fitting the description written by the Apostle Paul centuries earlier. (Ephesians 2:20.)

This day of organization was, in effect, a day of commencement, the graduation for Joseph from ten years of remarkable schooling. It had begun with the incomparable vision in the grove in the spring of 1820, when the Father and the Son appeared to the fourteen-year-old boy. It had continued with the tutoring from Moroni, with both warnings and instructions given on multiple occasions. Then there was the translation of the ancient record, and the inspiration, the knowledge, the revelation that came from that experience. There was the bestowal of divine authority, the ancient priesthood again conferred upon men by those who were its rightful possessors —John the Baptist in the case of the Aaronic Priesthood, and Peter, James, and John in the case of the Melchizedek. There were revelations, a number of them, in which the voice of God was heard again, and the channel of communication opened between man and the Creator. All of these were preliminary to that historic April 6.

A full century and a half have passed since that historic day. In ancient Israel, each fifty years was marked as a year of jubilee, a time for remembering, a time for gratitude, a time for generosity, a time to look about and assess the present and to look ahead and plan the future. For The Church of Jesus Christ of Latter-day Saints, this is indeed a time in which to look back with appreciation for all of those who have gone before us and made possible the miracle of the present, to look at our situation today with a spirit of accomplishment marked by humility, and to resolve to continue with enthusiasm and strong conviction the building of the mighty work which God himself restored in this the dispensation of the fulness of times.

Ours is an incomparable inheritance. What a terrible price has been paid for what we have today. There was much suffering even before 1830. There were the snide remarks, the cutting jeers, the vicious threats against the boy who declared that he had seen a vision both transcendent and wonderful. There was the crude laughter over "Joe Smith's gold Bible," with attempts to steal the sacred record. There was the heartbreaking loss of the 116 manuscript pages of the initial translation, the difficulty in finding a printer, the attempt of enemies to plagiarize the writing with a distorted version, the loss of the family home and farm through the knavish actions of a supposed friend. These and more were among the troubles of Joseph, the boy and the young man, through the years of his preparation.

And then followed the troubles that came like legions after the Church was organized. It was a long journey from the land of Cumorah to the valley of the Great Salt Lake as it was traveled in those early days, moving from place to place a cause and a kingdom and a people. Each location at first appeared as an oasis and subsequently became a place of despair. Repeatedly they arrived to search for peace, built for a season, and then were forced to leave, the objects of intolerance and persecution.

Kirtland, on the level land south of Lake Erie, was their first bright hope. Here they built their temple. This was a house of revelation, a spiritual refuge. But the peace of Kirtland was violated with tar and feathers, economic disaster, and blighted hopes. Missouri was next, rich with promise concerning a center stake of Zion. This was in fact to be Zion. That hope was blasted with rifle fire, the burning of homes, the cry of the night-riding mobs, death at Haun's Mill and Crooked River, the evil expulsion order, the painful march to the bottomlands of the Mississippi and over the river to a temporary asylum at Quincy. Left behind by the fleeing exiles was their prophet with a few associates in the jail at Liberty. There they spent the lonely, miserable months of the winter of 1838-39. It was here that Joseph cried out, "O God, where art thou?" (D&C 121:1.) Among the words of response came this remarkable prophecy:

"The ends of the earth shall inquire after thy name, and fools shall have thee in derision, and hell shall rage against thee; While the pure in heart, and the wise, and the noble, and the virtuous, shall seek counsel, and authority, and blessings constantly from under thy hand.

"And thy people shall never be turned against thee by the testimony of traitors." (D&C 122:1-3.)

There followed the miracle of Nauvoo, the City of Joseph. Here was the zenith of the prophet's mortal career—and the fast decline from that high point. The swamps were drained, a city planned, reaching from the water of the river up to the hill where the temple was built. The homes were of brick, sturdy and well planned. Sounds of industry were to be heard—sounds of hammer on anvil, of stone shaped by the masons' tools, of saw and lathe and plane. Beauty rose from that swampland, beauty and order and the society of Illinois' finest city. But there also rose a miasma of jealousy and hate and disloyalty. There were the Laws, the Higbees, the Bennetts, and others of their kind; and over in Missouri, Governor Boggs grew angry in his frustration over attempts to get at the Saints and more particularly their leader. Likewise politicians, concerned over the Mormon vote, did their part. Small problems became mountains of conflict. Joseph knew a storm was coming. Prophetically he said one day in Montrose that the Saints would continue to suffer much affliction, that they would be driven to the Rocky Mountains, and that there they would become a mighty people.

He never saw that day, except through the eyes of prophecy. June 27, 1844, was the hour of his tragedy. A mob, their faces blackened that sultry afternoon, took his life and that of his brother Hyrum. That night was the darkest of all the nights through which the Saints had lived in the city on the river. The forces of evil had finally claimed their prize. The Prophet was dead.

John Taylor, who had been with him at Carthage, summed up his work: "Joseph Smith, the Prophet and Seer of the Lord, has done more, save Jesus only, for the salvation of men in this world, than any other man that ever lived in it. . . . He lived great, and he died great in the eyes of God and his people." (D&C 135:3.)

Meanwhile the message of the restored gospel had been carried throughout the eastern states and Canada, and across the Atlantic to Britain. Notwithstanding the serious problems at home, converts came in ever-increasing numbers. Their strength was needed for the ordeals that lay ahead.

The first wagons rolled out in early February 1846. Later that month the river froze and the wagons were able to cross on the ice. But the same bitter weather that brought this boon also brought immense suffering to those who were leaving comfortable homes. There were no roads the way the Saints traveled, and as the ice melted, mud, deep and embracing, took its place. What a picture they were, these thousands of wagons strung along a thin line that reached from dying Nauvoo on the Mississippi to Council Bluffs coming alive on the Missouri, all across what is now the state of Iowa. There were births and deaths, each fraught with pain. On the west side of the Missouri a temporary city was built. It was called Winter Quarters. To those of lesser faith it might more fittingly have been named Despair. Nauvoo was irretrievably behind the exiles; to them it was the City of No Return. Their objective in the Rocky Mountains seemed so everlastingly far away, even beyond the length of life itself for many. They died and were buried in the little cemetery above the river—men, women, and children, the victims of exposure and cholera and black canker. Others traveling from the British Isles died at sea, or after coming up the river from New Orleans and getting as far as St. Louis, became victims to the dread disease that struck frequently, suddenly, and with finality.

But they sang a song in the strange land through which they moved—"Come, come, ye Saints, no toil nor labor fear;/But with joy wend your way." Its words spoke of courage, struggle, and death, but concluded always with the promise, "All is well! all is well!" (*Hymns*, no. 13.)

Another blow fell with the recruitment of the Mormon Battalion with five hundred of its badly needed strong young men, but they went with a promise, and without them the Saints began moving west the following spring. They broke their own trail, killing rattlesnakes by the cord, fording and ferrying the streams and rivers, pausing on the Sabbath to worship their God. They had left Winter Quarters when the warm spring sun melted the ice and grass began to green. They arrived in the valley of the Great Salt Lake in the scorching heat of summer when grass turned brown and withered from the absence of moisture.

But water from the mountain streams was turned onto the parched land, and for the first time plows broke the desert soil. The years that followed were years of struggle and expansion as they labored to make the desert blossom and to build Zion in the valleys. They requested no help from government, but unitedly worked to grub the sagebrush, to build canals, to lay out roads, and to erect temples and tabernacles, theaters and meetinghouses, schools and public buildings, as well as snug and comfortable homes. While doing all of this they expanded the work of carrying the gospel of salvation to the people of the earth, across their own America and Canada, over the sea to the British Isles and Europe, to the ancient lands of Asia and the South Pacific, and later to Mexico and Central and South America.

This is the great drama, with its own peculiar elements of tragedy and triumph, of a century and a half of The Church of Jesus Christ of Latter-day Saints. It is unique. It is heroic. It is tremendous. Notwithstanding the pressures of unrelenting persecution, the falsehood and vicious innuendo of public speakers and public press, the struggles against poverty and the harshness of nature, the Church and its people never took a step backward. There were pauses when it reeled from the blows of hate brought against it, but each year saw its membership grow in numbers and in strength. The predictions of its enemies evaporated without fulfillment. It outlived all of the prophets of doom who spoke against it.

I drafted these words while flying from Salt Lake City to Washington, D.C., with a telegram of invitation from the White House to attend a breakfast with the President of the United States and members of his cabinet, participating with a group of others from across the nation in a briefing to discuss critical issues facing the United States. I had been designated by President Spencer W. Kimball to represent him on this occasion.

Flying 600 miles an hour at 39,000 feet above sea level, I looked at the earth beneath me. I saw where my brethren and sisters of earlier generations broke the road along the Elkhorn and the Platte. I envisioned their wagons drawn in circles at night after traveling only fifteen or twenty miles in a long day. In my mind's eye I witnessed them nursing their sick and burying their dead. I heard the cries of widows and orphaned children, the sobs of unspeakable loneliness as shallow graves were dug by those who never again would visit those hallowed places. My journey completed, I entered the White House the next morning and sat among some of the wise of this nation, and reflected on the time when Joseph Smith also came to Washington, riding horseback much of the way and taking the cheapest lodging he could find, all that he could afford. He had come to make a plea for help from President Martin Van Buren, only to be rebuffed and return empty-handed to his people.

My journey epitomized for me the miraculous changes that have occurred since the days of Joseph. The little handful of people on April 6, 1830, has grown to more than 4.5 million. The provincialism of that beginning in the towns and villages of western New York has blossomed into a great cosmopolitan society established in seventy-two nations of the earth. The respect others presently have for the Church has been won over a period of many years through the integrity of our people.

Of course there are voices of dissent and still much of criticism. But these voices are like the barking of a little dog at the heels of a strong and beautiful animal. Some few pay attention to the barking, but most see above that noise to the innate strength, the solidarity, and the beauty of the creature at which its enemies shout their ineffective complaints.

Standing on the summit of a century and a half, we view with gratitude and humility what has been wrought. Prophecy has been fulfilled: "The mountain of the Lord's house [has been] established in the top of the mountains." Many people in many lands have said, "Let us go up to the mountain of the Lord, to the house of the God of Jacob; and he will teach us of his ways, and we will walk in his paths." (Isaiah 2:2-3.)

The Church today flourishes in a world of secularism. It is a refuge of spirituality to ever-increasing numbers. Not in the memory of any living member has the ratio of activity been so high. Increased faithfulness is evident in attendance at sacrament meetings, priesthood meetings, seminaries and institutes, and in temple attendance. Never before have there been so many missionaries, nor so many converts. Faithful and active members of the Church occupy positions of great trust in government, education, business, and the professions. Its building program is vast, yet there is difficulty in keeping up with the demands of growth. Growth, in fact, is its most serious challenge.

We are far from being a perfect society as we travel along the road to immortality and eternal life. The great work of the Church in furthering this process is to help men and women to move toward the perfection exemplified by the Savior of mankind. We are not likely to reach that goal in a day or a year or a lifetime. But as we strive in this direction, we shall become better men and women, sons and daughters of God.

Looking to the future, the challenges we see facing the Church are immense. The Lord himself has declared that this work will roll forth to fill the whole earth, in preparation for the coming of the Savior to reign as King of kings and Lord of lords. Much has been done, but much more remains to be done. All of the work of the past is but prelude to the work of the future. In lands where the gospel has been taught for a century and more, the numbers of the Saints are still relatively small. And in the earth's most populated nations the doors are presently closed. But somehow, under the power of the Almighty, they will in his time be opened, for this gospel "shall be preached in all the world for a witness unto all nations" before the end shall come. (Matthew 24:14.) There must be much more dedication, devotion, consecration. There must be a great expansion and a great acceleration.

Nor can we expect the powers of the adversary to lie dormant. Let us hope and pray that the days of burnings, drivings, and murders are forever behind us. But there will likely continue to be criticism and attacks of many kinds on the Church and its people. They will be of a more sophisticated nature than in the past; and in the future, as before, we may expect much of the criticism to come from those within the ranks of the Church—members of record while apostate in spirit. The very extent of the harassment we shall experience will stand as an evidence of the truth of this work. Else why would the adversary be so zealous to destroy it?

New challenges will arise as the work confronts new cultures. Yet there need be no fear of these. All of the people of the earth are sons and daughters of God, and there beats in the hearts of everyone something of divinity that will respond to the same teaching, no matter what the language or the land.

In days of sunshine it will become us to be humble. In times of storm we shall look to God for strength. This is his work. He will overrule for its blessing in the future as he has in the past. His Spirit will brood over the nations according to his will and wisdom, and hearts will be touched by its power.

The message of this work is the gospel of salvation. Its cause is the cause of peace. Its challenge lies in teaching eternal truths. Its victory lies in accomplishing the work of God.

19

JOSEPH THE SEER

Many of us have been gratified as we have read in periodicals and seen on television some complimentary references to the Church. For instance, one of the large-circulation magazines spoke appreciatively of the Mormon way of life, a way that discourages the use of tobacco, alcohol, tea, and coffee and encourages physical fitness. A network television broadcast reported on our tremendous genealogical program. There have been other positive accounts dealing with the organizational structure of the Church, with our welfare program, and with the family home evening program.

But largely absent from all of these accounts is any mention of the origin of these practices, or the reasons for them.

Further, some recent publications carry the thesis that there is nothing of the hand of Divinity in the establishment and development of the Church; that this has been only a natural response to contemporary social conditions.

An acquaintance said to me one day: "I admire your church very much. I think I could accept everything about it—except Joseph Smith." I responded: "That statement is a contradiction. If you accept the revelation, you must accept the revelator."

It is a constantly recurring mystery to me how some people speak with admiration for the Church and its work, while at the same time disdaining him through whom, as a servant of the Lord, came the framework of all that the Church is, of all that it teaches, and of all that it stands for. They would pluck the fruit from the tree while cutting off the root from which it grows.

The so-called Mormon code of health, widely praised in these days of cancer and heart research, is in reality a revelation given to Joseph Smith in 1833 as a "Word of Wisdom" from the Lord. (D&C 89:1.) In no conceivable way could it have come of the dietary literature of the time, nor from the mind of the man who announced it. Today, in terms of medical research, it is a miracle whose observance has saved incalculable suffering and premature death for uncounted tens of thousands.

Genealogical research is suddenly becoming a popular hobby as a result of Alex Haley's book *Roots*. Thousands of eyes across the world have been turned to what is described as the Mormon treasure house of genealogical data. But this tremendous program of the Church did not result from the pursuit of a hobby. It is an extension of the teachings of Joseph Smith, the Mormon prophet. He declared that we cannot be saved without our forebears, those who did not have a knowledge of the gospel and consequently could not fulfill its requirements nor partake of its opportunities.

The remarkable organization of the Church, which has received much attention, was framed by him as he was directed by revelation, and no modification or adaptation of that organization is ever considered without searching the revelations set forth by the Prophet.

Even the welfare program, which some are prone to regard as of rather recent origin, is founded and operated strictly upon principles enunciated by Joseph Smith in the early years of the Church. This is likewise true of the family home evening program, which is no more than an extension of early revelation on the responsibility of parents to bring up their children in "light and truth." (D&C 93:40.)

Some time ago, while riding in a plane, I engaged in conversation with a young man who was seated beside me. We moved from one subject to another, and then came to the matter of religion. He said that he had read considerably about the

Mormons, that he had found much to admire in their practices, but that he had a definite prejudice concerning the story of the origin of the Church and particularly Joseph Smith. He was an active member of another organization, and when I asked where he had acquired his information, he indicated that it had come from publications of his church. I asked what company he worked for. He proudly replied that he was a sales representative for IBM. I then asked whether he would think it fair for his customers to learn of the qualities of IBM products from a Xerox representative. He replied with a smile, "I think I get the point of what you're trying to say."

I took from my case a copy of the Doctrine and Covenants and read to him the words of the Lord through Joseph Smith, words that are the source of those practices my friend had come to admire in us while disdaining the man through whom they had come. Before we parted, he agreed to read the literature I would send to him. I promised him that if he would do so prayerfully, he would know the truth not only of these doctrines and practices which have interested him, but also of the man through whom they were introduced. I then gave him my testimony of my conviction concerning the prophetic calling of Joseph Smith.

We do not worship the Prophet. We worship God our Eternal Father, and the risen Lord Jesus Christ. But we acknowledge him, we proclaim him, we respect him, we reverence him as an instrument in the hands of the Almighty in restoring to the earth the ancient truths of the divine gospel, together with the priesthood through which the authority of God is exercised in the affairs of His church and for the blessing of His people.

The story of Joseph Smith's life is the story of a miracle. He was born in poverty. He was reared in adversity. He was driven from place to place, falsely accused, and illegally imprisoned. He was murdered at the age of thirty-eight. Yet in the brief space of twenty years preceding his death he accomplished what none other had accomplished in an entire lifetime. He translated and published the Book of Mormon, a volume of 522 pages that has since been retranslated into more than a score of languages and that is accepted by millions across the earth as the word of God. The revelations he received and other writings he produced are likewise scripture to these millions. The total in book pages constitutes the equivalent of almost the entire Old Testament of the Bible, and it all came through one man in the space of a few years.

In this same period he established an organization that for a century and a half has withstood every adversity and challenge, and that is as effective today in governing a worldwide membership of more than four and a half million as it was 150 years ago in governing a membership of a few thousand. There are those doubters who have strained to explain this remarkable organization as the product of the times in which he lived. That organization, I submit, was as peculiar, as unique, and as remarkable then as it is today. It was not a product of the times. It came as a revelation from God.

Joseph Smith's vision of man's immortal nature reached from an existence before birth to the eternities beyond the grave. He taught that salvation is universal in that all men will become the beneficiaries of the resurrection through the atonement wrought by the Savior. But beyond this gift is the requirement of obedience to the principles of the gospel and the promise of consequent happiness in this life and exaltation in the life to come.

Nor was the gospel he taught limited in application to those of his own and future generations. The mind of Joseph Smith, tutored by the God of heaven, encompassed all mankind of all generations. Both the living and the dead must have the opportunity to partake of gospel ordinances.

Peter of old declared: "For this cause was the gospel preached also to them that are dead, that they might be judged according to men in the flesh, but live according to God in the spirit." (1 Peter 4:6.) In the case of the dead there must be vicarious work if they are to be judged according to men in the flesh, and in order to accomplish this they must be identified; hence the great genealogical program of The Church of Jesus Christ of Latter-day Saints. It was not established to satisfy the interests of a hobby, but to accomplish the eternal purposes of God.

Within the space of that twenty years preceding his death, Joseph Smith set in motion a program for carrying the gospel to the nations of the earth. I marvel at the boldness with which he moved. Even in the infant days of the Church, in times of dark adversity, men were called to leave homes and families, to cross the sea, to proclaim the restoration of the gospel of Jesus Christ. His mind, his vision encompassed the entire earth.

When I was a boy, twelve years of age, my father took me to a meeting of the priesthood of the stake in which we lived. I sat on the back row while he, as president of the stake, sat on the stand. At the opening of that meeting, the first of its kind I had ever attended, three or four hundred men stood. They were men from varied backgrounds and many vocations, but each had in his heart the same conviction, out of which together they sang these great words:

> Praise to the man who communed with Jehovah!
> Jesus anointed that Prophet and Seer.
> Blessed to open the last dispensation,
> Kings shall extol him, and nations revere.
> —Hymns, no. 147

Something happened within me as I heard those men of faith sing. There came into my boyish heart a knowledge, placed there by the Holy Spirit, that Joseph Smith was indeed a prophet of the Almighty. In the many years that have since passed, years in which I have read much of his words and works, that knowledge has grown stronger and ever more certain. Mine has been the privilege of bearing witness across this nation from sea to shining sea, and on continents north and south, east and west, that he was and is a prophet of God, a mighty servant and testifier of the Lord Jesus Christ.

To a world plagued with doubt, Joseph Smith testified unequivocally of the risen, living Christ. That testimony was spoken in many ways and under many circumstances.

First, he spoke out of the experience of his incomparable vision of the Father and the Son, whom he both saw and heard. They were individual personages of form and substance, of body and voice. They spoke with him as one man speaketh with another.

Second, as the instrumentality through which came the Book of Mormon, Joseph Smith has borne witness of the Savior to all who have read and will read that volume. Its constantly recurring message is a testimony of the promised Messiah who came to the earth and gave his life for the sins of all mankind, and who rose triumphant from the grave as "the first fruits of them that slept." (1 Corinthians 15:20.)

Third, Joseph Smith bore witness of the living Lord through the church organized in this dispensation, even The Church of Jesus Christ of Latter-day Saints. This church carries the name of Jesus Christ, and its members are expected by precept and example to bear witness of him in whose name they meet and serve.

Fourth, Joseph Smith testified of the risen Lord when by the power of his prophetic office he spoke these remarkable words:

"And now, after the many testimonies which have been given of him, this is the testimony, last of all, which we give of him: That he lives!

"For we saw him, even on the right hand of God; and we heard the voice bearing record that he is the Only Begotten of the Father—

"That by him, and through him, and of him, the worlds are and were created, and the inhabitants thereof are begotten sons and daughters unto God." (D&C 76:22-24.)

Finally, he sealed that testimony with his life's blood, dying a martyr to the truths of which he had spoken concerning the Redeemer of the world, in whose name he had carried on his ministry.

> Great is his glory and endless his priesthood:
> Ever and ever the keys he will hold.
> Faithful and true, he will enter his kingdom,
> Crowned in the midst of the prophets of old.
> —Hymns, no. 147

20

"WE THANK THEE, O GOD, FOR A PROPHET"

We often sing in our meetings a marvelous hymn, a hymn we have sung for more than a century: "We Thank Thee, O God, for a Prophet." It is distinctive with us. As a people we sing some hymns that have come from other churches, and others sing some of ours. But only we can properly sing "We thank thee, O God, for a prophet to guide us in these latter days."

The hymn was written more than a century ago by a man of humble circumstances who lived in Sheffield, England. He worked in the steel mills and was discharged because he joined the Mormon Church. But there burned in his heart a great and fervent testimony; and out of an overflowing spirit of gratitude, he penned these marvelous lines. They have become a grateful expression of appreciation for millions over the earth. I myself have heard them sung in twenty-one different languages as a reverent prayer of thanksgiving for divine revelation.

How thankful we ought to be, how thankful we are, for a prophet to counsel us in words of divine wisdom as we walk our paths in these complex and difficult times. The solid assurance we carry in our hearts, the conviction that God will make his will known to his children through his recognized servant, is the real basis of our faith and activity. We either have a prophet or we have nothing; and having a prophet, we have everything.

Could any people have a greater blessing than to have standing at their head one who receives and teaches the will of God concerning them? We need not look far in the world to know that "the wisdom of their wise men" has perished, and that "the understanding of their prudent men" has come to naught. (Isaiah 29:14.) That wisdom for which the world should seek is the wisdom which comes from God. The only understanding that will save the world is divine understanding.

"Surely the Lord God will do nothing, but he revealeth his secret unto his servants the prophets." (Amos 3:7.)

It was so in the days of Amos and in all the years when holy men of God spoke as they were moved upon by the Holy Ghost. (See 2 Peter 1:21.) Those ancient prophets warned not only of things to come, but, more importantly, they became the revealers of truth to people. It was they who pointed the way men should live if they were to be happy and find peace in their lives.

I know a man who, as a Christian, trying one church after another, could find none that taught of a prophet. Only among the Jewish people did he find reverent mention of the prophets, and so he accepted and embraced the Jewish religion.

In the summer of 1964, he went to New York City and visited the World's Fair. He entered the Mormon Pavilion and saw pictures of the prophets of the Old Testament. His heart warmed within him as he heard the missionaries speak with appreciation of these great men of ages past through whom Jehovah revealed his will. Then, as he progressed through the pavilion, he heard of modern prophets—of Joseph Smith, who was called a prophet, a seer, and a revelator. Something stirred within him. His spirit responded to the testimony of the missionaries. He was baptized. He served a mission in South America, where he had many converts. He returned home and has since become the means of bringing his family and others into the Church. It is heartwarming to hear him testify that Joseph Smith was indeed a prophet of God and that all who succeeded him have been legal successors in this high and sacred calling.

Could anyone willing to read without bias the story of

Joseph Smith doubt that he was a great foreteller of events to come? Nearly thirty years before a shot was fired, he foretold the tragic American Civil War and stated that following that, war would be poured out upon all nations. You and I of this generation are witnesses to the fulfillment of those remarkable words.

He foretold that this people, then living in Illinois, would be driven out, would suffer much affliction, and would become a great and mighty people in the midst of the Rocky Mountains. The Church today, headquartered in Salt Lake City, is evidence of the fulfillment of those marvelous words of prophecy.

It has been so with his successors. On a cold winter day in 1849, when our forebears were hungry and living on sego roots and thistle tops, while gold was being found in California, Brigham Young stood in the old bowery on what is now Temple Square and spoke prophetic words to those who felt they might leave the hardships of life in the valley of the Great Salt Lake to go to greener pastures in California. Among other things, he said:

"We have been kicked out of the frying pan into the fire, out of the fire into the middle of the floor, and here we are and here we will stay. . . .

"We shall build a city and a temple to the Most High God in this place. We will extend our settlements to the east and the west, to the north and south, and we will build towns and cities by the hundreds, and thousands of saints will gather in from the nations of the earth.

"This will become the great highway of nations. Kings and emperors and the noble and the wise of the earth will visit us here. . . ."

How could anyone witness the hundreds of thousands, yes, the millions, who come each year to visit us, and have any doubt that Brigham Young spoke other than as a prophet? Over the years there has been a veritable parade of notables who have found their way to the office of the First Presidency, there to meet particularly the man whom we sustain as the president of the Church and as the prophet of our day. They include leaders in the governments of the earth, in business and commerce, in education, in the professions. These are among "the noble and the wise of the earth" of whom Brigham Young spoke when we were an outcast people, isolated in a mountain wilderness.

I am profoundly grateful not only for Joseph Smith as the prophet who served as an instrument in the hands of the Almighty in restoring this work, but also for all of those who have followed him. A study of their lives will reveal the manner in which the Lord has chosen them, has refined them, and has molded them to his eternal purposes. Joseph Smith declared on one occasion: "I am like a huge, rough stone rolling down from a high mountain . . . with all hell knocking off a corner here and a corner there, and thus I will become a smooth and polished shaft in the quiver of the Almighty."

He was hated and persecuted. He was driven and imprisoned. He was abused and beaten. And as you read his history, you see the evolution of which he spoke. There developed a power in his life. There came a refinement. There grew a love for others which even overcame his own love for life. The corners of that rough stone *were* knocked off, and he became a polished shaft in the hand of the Almighty.

It has been so with those who have succeeded him. Through long years of dedicated service, they have been refined and winnowed and chastened and molded for the purposes of the Almighty. Could anyone doubt this after reading the lives of such men as Brigham Young, Wilford Woodruff, Joseph F. Smith, and Spencer W. Kimball? The Lord subdued their hearts and refined their natures to prepare them for the great and sacred responsibility later thrust upon them.

As one to whom the Spirit has borne witness, I testify of their prophetic calling, and add my voice to the voices of our people over the earth, "We thank thee, O God, for a prophet to guide us in these latter days." I am grateful. I am satisfied that the peace and the progress and the prosperity of this people lie in doing the will of the Lord as that will is articulated by him who presides over this church. If we fail to observe his counsel, we repudiate his sacred calling. If we abide his counsel, we shall be blessed of God.

We ever pray for thee, our Prophet dear,
That God will give to thee comfort and cheer;
As the advancing years furrow thy brow,
Still may the light within shine bright as now.
                                        —Hymns, no. 386

God lives and is a revealer of eternal truth. Jesus Christ is our Savior and stands at the head of his church. We have a prophet upon the earth, a seer and a revelator to teach us. God give us the faith and the discipline within ourselves to follow that teaching.

21

WHY THESE TEMPLES?

Was there ever a man who, in a time of quiet introspection, has not pondered the solemn mysteries of life? Has he not asked himself: "Where did I come from? Why am I here? Where am I going? What is my relationship to my Maker? Will death rob me of the treasured associations of life? What of my wife and children? Will there be another existence after this, and if so, will we know one another there?"

The answers to these questions are not found in the wisdom of men. They are found only in the revealed word of God. Temples of The Church of Jesus Christ of Latter-day Saints are sacred structures in which these and other eternal questions are answered. Each is dedicated as a house of the Lord, a place of holiness and peace, shut apart from the world, where truths are taught and ordinances are performed that bring knowledge of things eternal and motivate the participant to live with understanding of his divine inheritance as a child of God and an awareness of his potential as an eternal being.

These buildings, different from the thousands of regular Church houses of worship scattered over the earth, are unique in purpose and function from all other religious edifices. It is not the size of these buildings nor their architectural beauty that makes them so. It is the work that goes on within their walls.

The designation of certain buildings for special ordinances, as distinguished from regular places of worship, is not new. This was the practice in ancient Israel, where the people worshipped regularly in the synagogues. Their more sacred place was, first, the tabernacle in the wilderness with its Holy of Holies, and then a succession of temples, where special ordinances were performed and where only those who met the required qualifications could participate in these ordinances.

So it is today. Prior to the dedication of a temple, The Church of Jesus Christ of Latter-day Saints invites the public to go through the building and inspect its various facilities. But when it is dedicated it becomes the house of the Lord, vested with a character so sacred that only members of the Church in good standing are permitted to enter. It is not a matter of secrecy. It is a matter of sanctity.

The work that goes on in these buildings sets forth God's eternal purposes with reference to man, God's child and creation. For the most part it is concerned with the family, with each of us as members of God's eternal family and with each of us as members of earthly families. It is concerned with the sanctity and eternal nature of the marriage covenant and family relationships.

It affirms that each man and woman born into the world is a child of God, endowed with something of his divine nature. The repetition of these basic and fundamental teachings has a salutary effect upon those who receive them. As the doctrine is enunciated in language both beautiful and impressive, the participant comes to realize that since every man is a child of a Heavenly Father, then each is a member of a divine family, and hence every man is his brother.

When asked by the scribe, "Which is the first commandment of all?" the Savior replied, "Thou shalt love the Lord thy God with all thy heart, and with all thy soul, and with all thy mind, and with all thy strength: this is the first commandment. And the second is like unto it, namely this, Thou shalt love thy neighbour as thyself." (Mark 12:28, 30-31.)

The teachings set forth in modern temples give powerful emphasis to this most fundamental concept of man's duty to his

Maker and to his brother. Sacred ordinances amplify this ennobling philosophy of the family of God. They teach that the spirit within each of us is eternal, in contrast with the body that is mortal. They not only give understanding of these great truths but also motivate the participant to love God and encourage him to demonstrate a greater neighborliness toward others of our Father's children.

If we accept the premise that man is a child of God, then there is divine purpose in mortal life. Here again, revealed truth is taught in the house of the Lord. Earth life is part of an eternal journey. We lived as spirit children before we came here. The scriptures bear testimony of this as witness the word of the Lord to Jeremiah: "Before I formed thee in the belly I knew thee; and before thou camest forth out of the womb I sanctified thee, and I ordained thee a prophet unto the nations." (Jeremiah 1:5.)

We come into this life as children of mortal parents and as members of families. Parents are partners with God in bringing to pass his eternal purposes with reference to his children. The family, therefore, is a divine institution, the most important both in mortality and in eternity.

Much of the work that goes on within temples is concerned with the family. Basic to an understanding of its meaning is recognition of the fact that even as we existed as children of God before we were born into this world, so also shall we continue to live after death, and the treasured and satisfying relationships of mortality, the most beautiful and meaningful of which are found in the family, may continue in the world to come.

Marriage partners who come to the house of the Lord and partake of its blessings are joined not only for the period of their mortal lives, but for all eternity, under authority not only of the law of the land that joins them until death parts them, but also of the eternal priesthood of God, binding in heaven that which is bound on earth. The couple so married has the assurance of divine revelation that their relationship and that of their children will not end with death, but will continue in eternity, provided they live worthy of that blessing.

Was there ever a man who truly loved a woman, or a woman who truly loved a man, who did not pray that their relationship might continue beyond the grave? Has a child ever been buried by parents who did not long for the assurance that their loved one would again be theirs in a world to come? Can anyone believing in eternal life doubt that the God of heaven would grant his sons and daughters that most precious attribute of life, the love that finds its most meaningful expression in family relationships? No, reason demands that the family relationships shall continue after death. The human heart longs for it. The God of heaven has revealed a way whereby it may be secured. The sacred ordinances of the house of the Lord provide for it.

But all of this would appear to be selfish indeed if the blessings of these ordinances were available only to those who are now members of The Church of Jesus Christ of Latter-day Saints. The fact is that the opportunity to come into the temple and partake of its blessings is open to all who will accept the gospel and be baptized into the Church. For this reason the Church carries forward an extensive missionary program in much of the world and will continue to expand this program as widely as possible, for it has the responsibility under divine revelation to teach the gospel to "every nation, kindred, tongue, and people."

But there are uncounted millions who have walked the earth and who have never had the opportunity to hear the gospel. Shall they be denied such blessings as are offered in the temples of the Church?

Through living proxies who stand in behalf of the dead, the same ordinances are available to those who have passed from mortality. In the spirit world they then are free to accept or reject those earthly ordinances performed for them, including baptism, marriage, and the sealing of family relationships. There must be no compulsion in the work of the Lord, but there must be opportunity.

This vicarious work constitutes an unprecedented labor of love on the part of the living in behalf of the dead. It makes necessary a vast undertaking of genealogical research to find and identify those who have gone before. To assist in this research, the Church coordinates a genealogical program and maintains research facilities unmatched in all the world. Its archives are open to the public and have been used by many who are not members of the Church in tracing their forebears. This program has been praised by genealogists throughout the world and has been utilized by various nations as a safeguard of their own records. But its primary purpose is to afford members of the Church the resources needed to identify their dead ancestors that they might extend to them the blessings that they themselves enjoy. They say to themselves, in effect, "If I love my wife and children so dearly that I want them for all eternity, then should not grandparents and other forebears have opportunity to receive the same eternal blessings?"

And so these sacred buildings are scenes of tremendous activity, quietly and reverently carried forward. They call to mind a part of the vision of John the Revelator wherein are recorded this question and this answer: "What are these which are arrayed in white robes? and whence came they?

"These are they which came out of great tribulation, and have washed their robes, and made them white in the blood of the Lamb. Therefore are they before the throne of God, and serve him day and night in his temple." (Revelation 7:13-15.)

Those who come to these holy houses are arrayed in white as they participate therein. They come only on recommendation of their local ecclesiastical authorities, having been certified as to their worthiness. They are expected to come clean in thought, clean in body, and clean in dress to enter the temple of God. As they enter they are expected to leave the world behind them and concentrate on things divine.

This very exercise, if such it may be called, carries with it a reward of its own, for who in these times of stress would not welcome an occasional opportunity to shut out the world and enter into the Lord's house, there to ponder quietly the eternal things of God? These sacred precincts offer the opportunity, available nowhere else, to learn of and reflect on the truly meaningful things of life—our relationship to Deity and our eternal journey from a preexistent state through this life and on to a future estate where we shall know and associate one with another, including our own loved ones and our forebears who have preceded us and from whom has come our inheritance of things of the body, mind, and spirit.

Surely these temples are unique among all buildings. They are houses of instruction. They are places of covenants and promises. At their altars we kneel before God our Creator and are given promise of his everlasting blessings. In the sanctity of their appointments we commune with him and reflect on his Son, our Savior and Redeemer, the Lord Jesus Christ, who served as proxy for each of us in a vicarious sacrifice in our behalf. Here we set aside our own selfishness and serve for those who cannot serve themselves. Here we are bound together in the most sacred of all human relationships—as husbands and wives, as children and parents, as families under a sealing that time cannot destroy and death cannot disrupt.

These sacred buildings were constructed even during those dark years when the Latter-day Saints were relentlessly driven and persecuted. They have been built and maintained in times of poverty and prosperity. They have come of the vital faith of an ever-growing number who bear witness of a living God, of the resurrected Lord, of prophets and divine revelation, and of the peace and assurance of eternal blessings to be found only in the house of the Lord.

22

THE MARRIAGE
THAT ENDURES

Springtime is the season when "a young man's fancy . . . turns to thoughts of love." (Alfred, Lord Tennyson, "Locksley Hall.") As an illustration, may I tell of two experiences.

The first happened when I was at the Washington (D.C.) Temple. A number of newsmen were present on that occasion. They were curious concerning that beautiful building, which is so different from other church buildings—different in concept, different in purpose, different concerning those who are permitted within its sacred precincts.

I explained that, after a temple building is dedicated as the house of the Lord, only members of the Church in good standing are authorized to enter, but that prior to its dedication, for a period of from a month to six weeks, visitors are made welcome to tour the entire structure; that we are not disposed to hide it from the world, but that, following the dedication, we regard it as being of so sacred a nature that purity of life and strict adherence to standards of the Church become qualifications for admittance.

We talked of the purposes for which temples are built. I explained those purposes, particularly emphasizing that purpose which appeals to all thoughtful men and women, namely, marriage for eternity. As I did so, I reflected on an experience at the time of the prededication showing of the London Temple in 1958.

On that occasion thousands of curious but earnest people stood in long lines to gain entry to the building. A policeman stationed to direct traffic observed that it was the first time he had ever seen the English eager to get into a church.

Those who inspected the building were asked to defer any questions until they had completed the tour. In the evenings I joined the missionaries in talking with those who had questions. As a young couple came down the front steps of the temple, I inquired whether I could help them in any way. The young woman spoke up and said, "Yes. What about this 'marriage for eternity' to which reference was made in one of the rooms?" We sat on a bench under the ancient oak that stood near the gate. The wedding band on her finger indicated that they were married, and the manner in which she gripped her husband's hand evidenced their affection one for another.

"Now to your question," I said. "I suppose you were married by the vicar."

"Yes," she responded, "just three months ago."

"Did you realize that when the vicar pronounced your marriage he also decreed your separation?"

"What do you mean?" she quickly retorted.

"You believe that life is eternal, don't you?"

"Of course."

I continued. "Can you conceive of eternal life without eternal love? Can either of you envision eternal happiness without the companionship of one another?"

"Of course not," came the ready response.

"But what did the vicar say when he pronounced your marriage? If I remember the language correctly, he said, among other things, 'in sickness and in health, for richer or for poorer, for better or for worse, till death do you part.' He went as far as he felt his authority would permit him, and that was till death separates you. In fact, I think that if you were to question him, he would emphatically deny the existence of marriage and family beyond the grave.

"But," I continued, "the Father of us all, who loves his

children and wants the best for them, has provided for a continuation, under proper circumstances, of this most sacred and ennobling of all human relationships, the relationships of marriage and family.

"In that great and moving conversation between the Savior and his apostles, wherein Peter declared, 'Thou art the Christ, the Son of the living God,' and the Lord responded, 'Blessed art thou, Simon Barjona: for flesh and blood hath not revealed it unto thee, but my Father which is in heaven,' the Lord then went on to say to Peter and his associates, 'And I will give unto thee the keys of the kingdom of heaven: and whatsoever thou shalt bind on earth shall be bound in heaven: and whatsoever thou shalt loose on earth shall be loosed in heaven.' (Matthew 16:13-19.)

"In that marvelous bestowal of authority the Lord gave to his apostles the keys of the holy priesthood, whose power reaches beyond life and death into eternity. This same authority has been restored to the earth by those same apostles who held it anciently, even Peter, James, and John." I continued by saying that following the dedication of the temple on the following Sunday, those same keys of the holy priesthood would be exercised in behalf of the men and women who came into that sacred house to solemnize their marriage. They would join in a union that death cannot dissolve and time cannot destroy.

Such was my testimony to this young couple in England. Such it is to all the world. Our Father in heaven, who loves his children, desires for them that which will bring them happiness now and in the eternities to come, and there is no greater happiness than is found in the most meaningful of all human relationships: the companionships of husband and wife and parents and children.

Some time ago I was called to the hospital bedside of a mother in the terminal stages of a serious illness. She passed away a short time later, leaving her husband and four children, including a little boy of six. There was sorrow, deep and poignant and tragic. But shining through their tears was a faith beautiful and certain that as surely as there was now a sorrowful separation, there would someday be a glad reunion, for that marriage had begun with a sealing for time and eternity in the house of the Lord under the authority of the holy priesthood.

Every man who truly loves a woman, and every woman who truly loves a man, hopes and dreams that their companionship will last forever. But marriage is a covenant sealed by authority. If that authority is of the state alone, it will endure only while the state has jurisdiction, and that jurisdiction ends with death. But add to the authority of the state the power of the endowment given by Him who overcame death, and that companionship will endure beyond life if the parties to the marriage live worthy of the promise.

When I was much younger and less brittle, we danced to a song whose words went something like this:

> *Is love like a rose*
> *That blossoms and grows,*
> *Then withers and goes*
> *When summer is gone?*

It was only a dance ballad, but it was a question that has been asked through the centuries by men and women who have loved one another and looked beyond today into the future of eternity.

To that question we answer no, and reaffirm that love and marriage under the revealed plan of the Lord are not like the rose that withers with the passing of summer. Rather, they are eternal, as surely as the God of heaven is eternal.

But this gift, precious beyond all others, comes only with a price—with self-discipline, with virtue, with obedience to the commandments of God. These may be difficult, but they are possible under the motivation that comes of an understanding of truth.

Brigham Young once declared: "There is not a young man in our community who would not be willing to travel from here to England to be married right, if he understood things as they are; there is not a young woman in our community, who loves the Gospel and wishes its blessings, that would be married in any other way." (*Discourses of Brigham Young*, p. 195.)

Many have traveled that far and even farther to receive the blessings of temple marriage. I have seen a group of Latter-day Saints from Japan who had denied themselves food to make possible the long journey to the Hawaii Temple. In London we met those who had gone without necessities to afford the 7,000-mile flight from South Africa to the temple in Surrey, England. There was a light in their eyes and smiles on their faces and testimonies from their lips that it was worth infinitely more than all it had cost.

And I remember hearing in New Zealand the testimony of a man from the far side of Australia who, having been previously sealed by civil authority and then joined the Church with his wife and children, had traveled all the way across that wide continent, then across the Tasman Sea to Auckland, and down to the temple in the beautiful valley of the Waikata. As I remember his words, he said, "We could not afford to come. Our worldly possessions consisted of an old car, our furniture, and our dishes. I said to my family, 'We cannot afford *not* to go. If the Lord will give me strength, I can work and earn enough for another car and furniture and dishes, but if I should lose these my loved ones, I would be poor indeed in both life and in eternity.' "

How shortsighted so many of us are, how prone to look only at today without thought for the morrow. But the morrow will surely come, as will also death and separation. How sweet is the assurance, how comforting is the peace that come from the knowledge that if we marry right and live right, our relationship will continue, notwithstanding the certainty of death and the passage of time. Men may write love songs and sing them. They may yearn and hope and dream. But all of this will be only a romantic longing unless there is an exercise of authority that transcends the powers of time and death.

Speaking in the Salt Lake Tabernacle many years ago, President Joseph F. Smith said, "The house of the Lord is a house of order and not a house of confusion; and that means . . . that there is no union for time and eternity that can be perfected outside of the law of God, and the order of his house. Men may desire it, they may go through the form of it, in this life, but it will be of no effect except it be done and sanctioned by divine authority, in the name of the Father and of the Son and of the Holy Ghost." (*Gospel Doctrine*, p. 272.)

In conclusion may I relate a story. It is fiction, but in principle it is true. Can you imagine two young people at a time when the moon is full and the roses are in bloom and a sacred love has matured between them? Johnny says to Mary, "Mary, I love you. I want you for my wife and the mother of our children. But I don't want you or them forever. Just for a season, and then goodbye." And she, looking at him through tears in the moonlight, says, "Johnny, you're wonderful. There's nobody else in all the world like you. I love you, and I want you for my husband and the father of our children, but only for a time, and then farewell."

That sounds foolish, doesn't it? And yet isn't that in effect what a boy says to a girl and a girl says to a boy in a proposal of marriage when they are given the opportunity of eternal union under "the new and everlasting covenant," but they choose to set it aside for a substitute that can last only until death comes?

Life is eternal. The God of heaven has also made possible eternal love and eternal family relationships.

God bless our dear young people that as they look forward to marriage, they may look not only for rewarding companionship and rich and fruitful family relationships through all of their mortal days, but to an even better estate where love and treasured associations may be felt and known under a promise given of God.

I bear witness of the living reality of the Lord Jesus Christ through whom this authority has come. I bear witness that his power, his priesthood, is among us and is exercised in his holy houses. Do not spurn that which he has offered. Live worthy of it and partake of it, and let the sanctifying power of his holy priesthood seal your companionship.

INDEX